D1626658

Peter Michel: Faith and Dogma
...or what the Pope didn't say

Peter Michel

Faith and Dogma

…or what the Pope didn't say

Bluestar
Communications

Woodside, California

This book was originally written in German. In translating the text to English, the editors have attempted to find and include the original English language source for all quoted material.

Translated by Petra Michel

First published in German under the title
Der Anti-Weltkatechismus
Christ-Sein in Liebe und Freiheit
©Aquamarin Verlag, Grafing, Germany 1995

This translation:
©1995 Bluestar Communications Corporation
44 Bear Glenn
Woodside, CA 94062
Tel: 800-6-Bluestar

Cover art by Raphael Kolley
Anglicized & Edited by Goddess Enterprises
Escondido, CA 92029

First printing 1995

ISBN: 1-885394-13-6

Michel, Peter, 1953—
    [Anti-Weltkatechismus. English]
    Faith and dogma—or what the Pope didn't say / Peter Michel
        p.   cm.
    Includes bibliographical references.
    ISBN 1-885394-13-6
    1. Catholic Church—Doctrines—Controversial literature.
    2. Catholic Church. Catechismus Ecclesiae Catholicae—
    Controversial literature. 3. Occultism. I. Title
    BX1765.2.M4913   1995
    238'.2—dc20

Printed in the USA

Contents

He who accepts a new paradigm at an early stage must have faith that the new paradigm can cope with the many problems with which it will be confronted, knowing only that the old paradigm has failed him in some cases. A decision of this kind can be made only on the basis of faith.

THOMAS KUHN

Preface

The new Catechism of the Catholic Church, or the Catholic Catechism for short, is eight hundred and three pages long in the English edition. One might think that a critique such as Faith and Dogma should be a volume of comparable length. I have no doubt that some day such a studious scientific discourse will be available to assist a generation of academics. It is sure to list a myriad pros and cons in the development and advancement of its thesis. Lengthy commentaries will be written, with innumerable footnotes, and with page after page of bibliography. The question remains, however, as to who is going to read these volumes? Most likely it will be the members of a small, elitist theological body rather than the many faithful seekers from small communities dotted across the globe.

At the conclusion of the Twentieth Century, a person striving to find religious direction and seeking answers to his many burning questions does not wish to wade through thirty pages of text to find out whether or not there is a Hell.

In our times, religion is no longer a matter of "shepherds and sheep." This may have been an appropriate description for the Third Century but it certainly does not characterize present-day religious life. In this sense, the intrinsic philosophy of the Catholic Catechism is a philosophy oriented toward the past, where the "shepherd" (the Pope) shows the way and the "sheep" are to follow obediently. This attitude is manifest to a frightening extent in John Paul II's book *Crossing the Threshold of Hope*, where the patronizing condescension of journalist Vittorio Messori, whose questions form the basis for the Pope's book, is even more unbearable.

In that book, Religion is not understood to be a partnership or a brotherly search for truth and religious experience but is viewed rather as a hierarchical pronouncement of prescribed, obligatory dogma, which must be adhered to unequivocally.

With this form of religion there cannot be "seekers" in the truest sense of the word, for the answers are already known and the *'experiences'* are meticulously prescribed. Should one's *actual experiences* deviate from those prescribed, religious righteousness/correctness is endangered. Moreover, should such experiences be made public, the Roman 'power house' will apply its entire instrumentation with uncompromising tenacity. Men such as Teilhard de Chardin, Küng, Boff, Fox or Drewermann, to mention but a few, have experienced the firm and painful grip of dogmatic rule in this century. Confrontation and suppression characterize the language of Rome. No trace of the spirit of loving tolerance and spiritual freedom can be found.

Freedom, love and tolerance, however, form the foundation upon which the work that follows must be built. At this point, perhaps I should mention that this book is in no way intended to be adversarial. It is not my intention to write against the Catechism of the Catholic Church *per se*. Rather, this work is an attempt to present a critical examination of the thoughts of Esoteric Philosophy as a possible and viable alternative—an "esoteric" or "mystical philosophy" which has been present as a hidden line of tradition throughout history and which has occasionally become evident in the works of the mystics of all world religions. From the Vedic Rishis to the Egyptian Hierophants, traditional lines lead to the Greek mystery schools and the mysterious figure of Ammonios Saccas in Alexandria during the Third Century. It is therefore not surprising that Plotinus, the founder of neoplatonism, and Ammonios are viewed by esoteric traditions as the embodiment of those masters who, behind the veil of time, have guided the evolution of mankind on earth as "older brothers and sisters" as it were. Frequently, these great sages shape the world's fate with invisible hands, their work sometimes carried on by their students. It is rare in history to find these initiates, these wise men and women, met with understanding in their own time; only too often they were considered heretics or fell victim to priesthood intrigues. Meister Eckhart and Giordano Bruno are two such cases. Some of these people lit up the darkness like a flare, only to be extinguished as quickly as they appeared. Such a soul was Novalis.

Many changes have taken place over the past one-hundred and fifty years. With the onset of systematic research into oriental traditions, from as far back as the German Romantic Period, both interest in and knowledge of the Asian teachings of wisdom have grown. Decisive developments took place during the last quarter of the Nineteenth Century. In 1875, Helena P. Blavatsky and Henry S. Olcott founded the Theosophical Society in New York and 1893 saw the first convention of the World Parliament of Religions in Chicago, with a legendary address given by Vivekananda, the most prominent student of the great Indian saint Ramakrishna. A new phase of encounters among all world religions began and the esoteric tradition was taken from the shadows of its hidden existence into the light of public awareness. This was an exciting time of revolutionary ideas, yet it had its own delusions and pseudo-mystical ripples of infatuation. But the seed had been planted and the Twentieth Century, although the bloodiest in the history of mankind, was to reap a rich spiritual harvest. The esoteric communities, especially the Theosophical Society, the Anthroposophical Society and numerous Rosicrucian groups, as well as several outstanding mystics and wise men and women, opened completely new horizons to the seeking Christian and the long-buried paths to their own mystical traditions became accessible to all.

Sri Aurobindo discovered new levels of understanding within the Indian tradition of wisdom; Lama Anagarika Govinda and the XIVth Dalai Lama brought Tibetan Buddhism to the West; Pir Vilayat Khan earned Sufiism new recognition in the West; Martin Buber and Gershom Scholem initiated seekers into the mysterious depths of Chassidism and the Cabbala, and Flower A. Newhouse proclaimed the living Cosmic Christ and the world of angels. At their side Krishnamurti appeared, a figure who challenged religious orthodoxy with "the sword of discernment" to lead mankind to inner freedom.

All these important spiritual figures have shaped what I refer to simply as Esoteric Philosophy, so as to avoid having to describe each distinct traditional line in each individual case. Since there is no such thing as *the* Esoteric Philosophy as a firmly established (dogmatic!) teaching, this terminology should only be considered as a collective noun.

We truly live in a "time of change!" The religious person of today no longer thinks primarily in a denominational way. He is open to the wisdom of the world and the messages of sages from any country and from any tradition. For this reason, the Catechism of the Catholic Church must be examined critically to determine whether or not it is capable of permitting dialogue.

Each reader may then decide individually whether or not to seek the dialogue and to pursue it. This is the only viable approach to religious debate today, an approach that Hans Küng has undertaken in his recent great work *Christianity—Nature and History*.

Finally, a personal remark concerning both subject and method. As mentioned before, nothing is further from my heart and mind than to offend the personal religious beliefs of Catholics. When I challenge the Catechism of the Catholic Church, in its essence, it is never with disrespect to religious belief *per se* but is rather in the nature of a critical comparison. In fact, I believe that I take the Catechism of the Catholic Church more seriously than a great number of Catholics, a number of whom scoffed at my book project with the comment that no one picks up the Catechism anyway. In my opinion, every Catholic should either espouse support of "religious obedience" as dictated by the Catechism of the Catholic Church—or should leave the Church.

In the following treatise I do not refer directly to any particular esoteric teaching or specific author. I am concerned solely with the material itself, its readability and clarity. The interested reader who wishes to learn more about esoteric sources may refer to the publications listed in the bibliography and to additional critical publications on the subject of the history of the Church and its dogma.

CHAPTER 1

God

The tao that can be told
is not the eternal Tao.
The name that can be named
is not the eternal Name.

LAO TSE

"All creatures bear a certain resemblance to God, most especially man, created in the image and likeness of God." (§41)[†]

"Through an utterly free decision, God has revealed himself and given himself to man. This he does by revealing the mystery, his plan of loving goodness, formed from all eternity in Christ, for the benefit of all men. God has fully revealed this plan by sending us his beloved Son, our Lord Jesus Christ, and the Holy Spirit." (§50)

The fundamental premise of Esoteric Philosophy has always been to take God's absolute holiness seriously and with great reverence. Yet it is entirely unimportant whether this infinite holiness bears the name God, Brahman, Tao, Allah, Ain Soph, Nirvana or any

---

[†] The Catechism of the Catholic Church is quoted with its respective paragraph number. Italics, etc. correspond to the style in the Catechism.

other name. The great seers and sages of all times have seen the LIGHT that gives life to all that is, all that has been, and all that will be. They immersed themselves in this LIGHT, which transformed them; they knew immediately that they had touched the rim of God. "Into the light you shall enter, but its flame you shall never touch," goes the old aphorism.

The mystics have always emphasized the resemblance between the Creator and His creatures, although not in the literal sense of Genesis. There is an affinity in spirit—in the essence of all creatures—which must not be limited to the human form. The particular importance of this will unfold later on, in the context of the body-soul problem.

Spiritual evolution will lead all life in ever growing spirals to a deeper understanding of the divine mystery and so lead to a more profound revelation. As a being becomes more filled with the LIGHT, it may reveal the LIGHT with increasing brightness. Never has Esoteric Philosophy presumed, however, that there might be a *final* realization. The changeable can never recognize the whole of the Unchangeable; the created can never recognize all of the Uncreated.

The great seers (Sri Aurobindo, for example) tried to clothe what they had seen with new words. They attempted to let the absolute transcendence—the 'One Beyond Being'—shine forth in all its magnificence. Aurobindo spoke of the "supramental" or of the "supracosmic Para-Brahman," always motivated by the intention of having the unseen Unfathomable shine forth from the seen Unfathomable. No one was more humble than those great in spirit who truly knew of what they spoke when they gave an account of God's splendor.

Therefore, it is not possible to speak of "revealing the mystery of God." Every revelation—as well as any Christian revelation—occurs in its own time; the evolution of consciousness within its respective historical era determines and colors it. Every son and daughter of God unveils *an* innermost secret of God, knowing that there might be much more to say, although incomprehensible to others in his or her time. He is, and this is the tragic fate of all of God's sons and daughters, limited in two ways. His younger brothers and sisters in the evolutionary process can understand him merely at their own level of maturity; the mission of his incarnation limits his progress in SPIRIT. The coming of all sons and daughters of God is an indescribable sacrifice, having to descend from the magnificence and the unlimited realm of spirit to the darkness and limited realm of matter.

Even at the conclusion of the Twentieth Century, the Catholic Catechism does not incorporate a cosmic dimension in its image of God. Its image of God, the world, and humanity is frighteningly geocentric. It views the earth—this beautiful speck of dust in the universe—as the locus for God's complete revelation. This is the chosen site to which, according to an *eternal* plan, God has sent His *only begotten* son to save the fallen "specks of dust" on this "speck of dust." People who know the esoteric teachings can only wonder about the ignorant arrogance of the *Catechists* who seem to imagine themselves as the chosen on a chosen planet.

About the absolute spirit we can merely say, "HE is." All the descriptions of the seers and mystics speak only of his LIGHT and his LOVE. Concealed in HIM are innumerable worlds and solar systems; they encompass an infinite diversity of life forms—many of which are the Buddhas and Christs of their own distant realms. Wherever life exists, Love and Compassion summon God's sons and daughters to perform healing and redeeming work. Wherever these shining messengers appear, they proclaim the splendor, the magnificence of the ONE; all revelations remain merely shadows in the face of the ABSOLUTE LIGHT.

CHAPTER 2

God's Revelation

Not even a person of the highest realization has arrived at the highest level of insight. We are all on the ladder of evolution. Even the highest cannot arrive at an absolute truth, at the Spirit of the World. And even upon arrival at a higher level of realization, our judgment is still relative, yet ever-expanding, when we have reached a yet higher peak.

RUDOLF STEINER

"Christ, the son of God made man, is the Father's one, perfect, and unsurpassable Word. In him he has said everything; there will be no other word than this one." (§65)

"Christian faith cannot accept any 'revelations' that claim to surpass or to correct the Revelation of which Christ is the fulfillment, as is in the case in certain non-Christian religions and also in certain recent sects which base themselves on such 'revelations'." (§67)

One must read with care to comprehend fully and clearly the statement in the above two quotations. According to these statements *humans* anchor the framework within which God's revelations must take place! Humans lift themselves to heights where they presume to dictate action even to God. Of course, these people would reply to this objection that they merely attempt to interpret God's revelation; such a disclaimer cannot alter the facts. Two thousand years after Christ's incarnation, a few individuals decide what 'revelation' was, is, or will be (or rather, will *not* be). Their disdain of other revelations reveals the authors' mental bias.

The Pope strengthens their position in one of his recent books. "This Revelation is *definitive;* one can only accept it or reject it." (JP, p.10)[†]

Two thousand years of spiritual search have brought an immense wealth of insight into the mystery of life. The Pope simply interprets this eon with benevolence; he characterizes it as being of—at most—secondary importance. Over thousands of years, the Indian Yogis, Buddhist Lamas, Jewish Cabbalists or Islamic Sufis bestowed on humanity all the gifts of wisdom; to the Roman dogmatists, all of these insights are merely sound and smoke. There is hardly any other context in which the incompetence and unwillingness of the Catholic Church to act as an ecumenist for the world is more evident. Those who claim sole proprietorship of all the knowledge and all the wisdom of all times, and therefore the absolute and ultimate revelation, wholly oppose any form of religious dialogue. The unyielding grip of this attitude throughout the centuries is evident in a single glance at the history of the Christian mission. It has never been a mission of dialogue. Rather, it has always been a mission with an aim to convert (not to mention the terrible extent to which it has been a mission of sword and blood).

When religion, any form of religion, takes such a rigid, fundamentalist position, it becomes one of the determining forces

---

[†] John Paul II's book is quoted as "JP",with a corresponding page number.

in the division of people. The history of religious wars throughout the ages and even to this day provides sufficient evidence of this fact. Religious fundamentalism almost always leads to inquisitorial intolerance, should there ever be such an opportunity in a secular society. Comprehending this danger and being aware of the limitless nature of God's revelation, Esoteric Philosophy emphasizes the necessity for religious dialogue. To the mystics, the walls between the religions do not reach to the sky. They look beyond it and find brothers and sisters in SPIRIT. Wherever the divine light finds a pure heart it lights a flame. Each of these flames is a light in the world and yet often the world does not recognize this.

When the Dalai Lama and the Benedictine mystic Bede Griffiths, the Sufi master Pir Vilayat, or the Zionist Teddy Kollek speak together, none of these men would ever try to convert the other. Men and women, brothers and sisters in spirit, converse with one another and share their knowledge for the benefit of the whole of the human family.

Humanity must engage in religious dialogue as a life principle—as a search for understanding the other's wisdom—or the masses of fundamentalists will eventually trample down everything and probably establish dictatorships of intolerance. Dictatorships in which weapon—fixated 'religious' systems will confront one another to validate the superiority of their God through military victory. We can only hope that history will not repeat itself in this way. Acknowledging the truth and the reality of the revelations of other religions is a necessary first step in this direction.

Chapter 3

The Bible

Freedom means leaving traditions behindand experimenting.

KRISHNAMURTI

"*Sacred Scripture* is the speech of God as it is put down in writing under the breath of the Holy Spirit." (§81)

"For Holy Mother Church, relying on the faith of apostolic age, accepts as sacred and canonical the books of the Old and the New Testaments, whole and entire, with all their parts, on the grounds that, written under the inspiration of the Holy Spirit, they have God as their author and have been handed on as such to the Church herself." (§105)

"The Church receives from the Gospel the full revelation of the truth about man." (§2419)

The questionable nature of these statements is obvious to every open-minded individual. An unbiased examination of a mere two centuries of critical theology is sufficient to refute any thesis of "divine verbal inspiration." The oldest fragments of the gospels are Greek papyri from the Second Century, which even then were copies of copies and which date back to about one hundred years after the originals, whatever these originals may have looked like.

At the end of the Fourth Century, Jerome compiled the *Vulgate,* a version of the Old Testament and New Testament still in use in the Roman Church today. Pillars of the church disputed this document for centuries and it was not accepted until 1546 at the Council of Trent. This council, as well as the Council of Florence in 1442, determined the Bible's inspirational teaching that the Vatican Council of 1870 subsequently accepted as dogma. Even for a number of Catholic theologians, all this represented an unreasonable falsification of history and led Pius X to his 1907 attempt to silence the critical voices within the Church by means of both a *syllabus* and an *encyclica* condemning Modernism.[†]

Truth, however, cannot be suppressed by force for long. The true history of the New Testament's development is known well, even in Catholic circles. However, there is a difference between simply being known and being known *and* made public. Therefore, someone who wants to pursue a career in the Roman Catholic Church should never cite nor speak certain knowledge; church veterans give this piece of advice openly, even in Rome itself.

The gospels surely breathe the spirit of Christ, regardless of who compiled them or when they were written. They help us to understand the majesty of a wonderful, heavenly messenger whose profound message unfolds gradually before us, for only the wise understand the wise—even the Holy Spirit itself may enter only where the soul is ready.

To assume that the Church has received "full revelation of the truth about man" through the gospels requires a religious seeker to accept that all other realizations about the nature of mankind,

---

[†] Modernism is a movement within the Church which attempts to reinterpret some of the aspects of Catholithism in terms of the modern intellectual world.

delivered throughout the following millennia, are largely insignificant.

Each era possesses a certain knowledge, though often incomplete, since not all existing knowledge is available universally during any one era. Over the centuries, some knowledge was lost—only to be rediscovered and reorganized later. One should generally observe from the ongoing process of evolution that the present era possesses more knowledge of human nature than was known in the time of Thomas Aquinas.

The biblical text is inspiring, but is not inspired. It bears witness to the life and work of Christ, yet the witness is mankind. Therefore Luke, in the preface to the gospel bearing his name, was simply being honest when he wrote: "Since many have undertaken to set an orderly account of the events that have been fulfilled among us, just as they were handed on to us by those who from the beginning were eyewitnesses and servants of the word, I too decided, after investigating everything carefully from the very first, to write an orderly account for you, most excellent Theophilus, so that you may know the truth concerning the things about which you have been instructed."

Luke was no exception to the task of "carefully investigating" everything, of selecting and examining, since he could not be sure that the Holy Spirit was present to guide his pen.

CHAPTER 4

The Magisterium of the Church

Not only in the Old Testament one finds the killing letter; even in the New Testament one finds this letter that destroys whoever does not comprehend the spiritual meaning of what has been said.

ORIGEN

"'The task of giving an authentic interpretation of the Word of God, whether in its written form or in the form of Tradition, has been entrusted to the living, teaching office of the Church alone. Its authority in this matter is exercised in the name of Jesus Christ.' This means that the task of interpretation has been entrusted to the bishops in communion with the successor of Peter, the Bishop of Rome." (§85)

"The Church's Magisterium exercises the authority it holds from Christ to the fullest extent when it defines dogmas, that is, when it proposes truths contained in divine Revelation or having a necessary connection with them, in a form obliging the Christian people to an irrevocable adherence of faith." (§88)

"The redemption is the source of the authority that Christ, by virtue of the Holy Spirit, exercises over the Church." (§669)

These cogent words must convince even the last wavering believer what the issue is really all about. Doubt in the Church and its teachings means doubt in Christ. Christ and the Church are one; without the Church there is no salvation. It requires genuine, titanic boldness and an infallible mechanism for repression to make such demands of a follower after two thousand years of religious history.

This monumental and unrealistic position manifests itself in the Pope's assessment of the significance of the Catholic Catechism.

"And interest in the Catechism continues. We find ourselves faced with a new reality. *The world, tired of ideology, is opening itself to the truth.*" (JP, p.164)

Reports of congregations throughout the world accepting the Catholic Catechism do not seem to reach the Pope; clearly, sales figures do not equate to agreement.

It is helpful that the Church's statements are clear regarding its opposition to free choice. To the Catholic believer, Rome presents dogma in an absolute binding form, calling for "an irrevocable adherence of faith." One cannot stress strongly enough the finality of this proclamation. Dogma is "irrevocable." It is not only eternal truth, it also defines clearly what one must believe and what one must reject. It is binding and demands absolute obedience to the Church.

Esoteric Philosophy shares none of these ideas. There is no dogma, since there is no one who could offer a binding definition. Everybody is seeking, so only individuals can find truths. Others may also find them and so a particular view of life takes shape. It obligates no one and never demands "an irrevocable adherence of faith." Since the esoteric view of life is dynamic, it does not coerce obedience. Whom would such obedience benefit in any case? There is no power structure—no palace—to defend; even if such structures did exist, one would not find Esoteric Philosophy connected to them.

The Church and only the Church, headed by the Pope, has the divine trust of the authentic interpretation of God's word. The Pope clings to this view adamantly; those who know about the Roman Catholic Church and do not join it cannot attain salvation [see JP, pp.108-109]. If we study carefully the history of some dogmas, from the Trinity to infallibility, doubt in the divine guidance of this Church becomes practically inescapable; however, the real tragedy becomes fully evident only after we try to imagine what it means for the Church to exercise the "authority it holds from Christ to the fullest extent." One may look at examples, such as the Alexandrine philosopher Hypatia (cruelly torn to shreds in 416 by the Christian mob), or her spiritual brother Giordano Bruno (burnt in Rome in 1600), or at unnamed masses of heretics and witches. The flow of blood for which the 'Church of Christ' is responsible fills entire oceans. All of these horrible events are unspeakable treason to the message of Christ. Throughout the Catholic Catechism, not a single word of regret, no mention—no confession of guilt asking forgiveness—is evident. The strongest expression of the slightest insight lies in the phrase "regrettable facts."

One can hardly believe the words contained in §2298: "In times past, cruel practices were commonly used by legitimate governments to maintain law and order, often without protest from the Pastors of the Church, who themselves adopted in their own tribunals the prescriptions of Roman law concerning torture. Regrettable as these facts are, the Church always taught the duty of clemency and mercy. She forbade clerics to shed blood. In recent times it has become evident that these cruel practices were neither necessary for public order, nor in conformity with the legitimate rights of the human person. On the contrary, these practices led to ones even more degrading. It is necessary to work for their abolition. We must pray for the victims and for their tormentors." (§2298)

This passage overflows with historical lies. Even Catholic historians referred to the infamous Tenth Century of ecclesiastic history as "a century of darkness." From any perspective it is a virtual mockery of the victims. One must carefully read the sentences word by word in order not to overlook anything. The "cruel practices" occurred "in times past" under "legitimate governments"—of course—to maintain "law and order." The last of the witch trials and burnings took place in Catholic Bavaria during the second half of the Eighteenth Century! *"Under explicit orders from the Church"* ought to replace "without protests from the Pastors of the Church." The "adopting Roman law concerning torture" in no way reflects the treacherous perfection of the Church's destructive mechanisms during the Inquisition. Pope Innocence VIII's Bull in 1484 and its effect, the *Malleus Maleficarum*, "The Hammer of Evildoers," written by the Dominican inquisitors Heinrich Insistoris and Jakob Sprenger in 1489, resulted in the torture and death of hundreds of thousands of innocent victims. Truly these are "regrettable facts" in the framework of a church supporting "clemency and mercy." One would certainly hope that "in recent times" a better insight *has* taken its place.

Untouched by nearly two thousand years and—at least to a large extent—characterized by the cruelest forms of suppression, the First Vatican Council blessed the Church "for her marvelous propagation, eminent holiness, and inexhaustible fruitfulness in everything good…" (§812)

More appropriately, the Benedictine Bede Griffiths wrote a letter from his ashram during April of 1991. "The history of the

Inquisition with regard to imprisonment, torture and burning of heretics can be compared only to present time actions of Hitler and Stalin."

All these events would be *merely* tragic history had they not been carried out by an organization that claims to be the sole, exclusive, and lawful interpreter and administrator of God's Word. Millions of dead and rivers of blood "in the name of" and "by the authority of" He who was the absolute incarnation of love. Has there ever been greater treachery in the history of mankind?

CHAPTER 5

Religious Obedience

For God has not made mankind's salvation dependent on some special way...and this is how people should notice that they are doing wrong: when they occasionally see or hear mention a good person who does not follow their way, they immediately think all is lost (for them). If they dislike this way, they do not respect the good way or good intentions either. This is not right!... It is not possible that there be only one way for everyone; neither can all have just one way, nor can one have all ways or everyone's way.

MEISTER ECKHART

"To obey (from the Latin *ob-audire* to 'hear or to listen to') in faith is to submit freely to the word that has been heard, because its truth is guaranteed by God, who is Truth itself." (§144)

"Believing is possible only by grace and the interior helps of the Holy Spirit. But it is no less true that believing is an authentically human act." (§154)

Classical circular reasoning is used to justify 'religious obedience': The Church preaches the 'word;' the word is Truth, since it is from God; naturally, one must obey God, therefore one must obey the Church. However, if only one link in this chain of reasoning is faulty, the entire chain breaks. The Church has obviously proclaimed any number of erroneous statements and made its share of mistakes, so that *blind* religious obedience is unjustifiable. It seems more reasonable to examine everything and to keep the best.

Esoteric Philosophy differentiates the various meanings of faith. On the one hand, it understands faith to be an inner certainty that one is safe in God—a form of basic trust unbound by any dogma. On the other hand, it rejects any form of blind religious obedience as dangerous (due to the possibility of abuse) and as against reason. "Do not believe something simply because the Buddha has said so," taught Gautama. God's messengers do not demand blind faith, for this would profoundly contradict the premise of the individual's freedom. However, when one takes into account the Pope's dismissive remarks concerning the idea of freedom (JP, p.50), one can no longer regard even this idea as a general basis for human values.

Moreover, the esoteric traditions reject the idea that one should "submit oneself freely to the word that has been heard." Instead, they adhere to the importance of transforming 'the word' into an inner meaning and realizing it in full freedom, in one's daily life. A child of God whose face reflects the truth walks upright on the spiritual path, rather than crawling in subordination.

The abuse of good faith throughout history has caused some esoteric teachers to use doubt as the central principle for understanding. Only the critical questioning and weighing of a situation can discern the truth from what is false; a form of questioning which must not be mistaken for despair. In this case it is constructive, creative questioning and not blind faith, it is rather a careful examination intended to arrive at a position of agreement or disagreement.

Besides this critical attitude, the esoteric teachings also advocate the concept of trust. A teacher, tested over many years, has proven himself to be true and good. He may make a statement about some fact that the student cannot comprehend at the time; the teacher's benefit of doubt (trust) will extend as far as the student follows his teacher's path; based on the student's own experience, one can someday find the truth for oneself.

The esoteric teachings and the Catholic Catechism agree that both faith *and* its realization require grace. However, grace is considered to be a *cosmic* event. It is never limited to special, *select* religious communities.

Numberless paths may lead a seeker to approach the truth, all the while believing or doubting, yet always kept safe by virtue of grace. The choice between accepting or rejecting lies within the province of one's inner freedom. The very core of one's divine nature offers the guarantee of one day reaching the end of this search.

CHAPTER 6

The Trinitarian Dogma

*If you loved me you would rejoice that I am going
to the Father, because the Father is greater than I.*
JESUS OF NAZARETH (JOHN 14:28)

"The Trinity is One. We do not confess three Gods, but one
God in three persons, the 'consubstantial Trinity' [Council of
Constantinople II, 553]. The divine persons do not share the
one divinity among themselves but each of them is God whole
and entire: 'The Father is that which the Son is, the Son that
which the Father is, the Father and the Son that which the Holy
Spirit is, i.e., by nature one God.'" [Council of Toledo XI, 675]
(§253)

Hardly any other dogma of the Catholic Church has been more
hotly debated throughout history than the Trinitarian Dogma.
Minds have differed on teachings about the Trinity, from
Origen's subordination theory to criticism of Drewermann's
picture of Jesus.

   In many respects, the early Church did not think in Trinitarian
terms. It considered Christ a divine messenger, a higher being,
or an angel. In Origen's view—as well as later in the view of
Arius—the Son was inferior to the Father. Various groups had

formed before the Council of Nicaea convened in 325. These groups occasionally engaged in furious dispute. Through the strict intervention of Emperor Constantine (who did not want any disputes with the Church for political reasons), the bishops had to accept a formula that, until then, none of the disputing groups had ever advocated: *homo-ousios*, the equal essence of the Father and of the Son. This new dogma remained the focus of dispute for a long time and was the subject of vehement argument during the so-called Arian controversies; I shall not pursue the history of theology further here, but Küng and Panikkar provide valuable insight into this topic.

The esoteric traditions do not dispute Christ being a Son of God in any way; they merely dispute the idea of Christ being the *only* Son of God, as the Pope quite explicitly states: "Christ is absolutely original and absolutely unique." (JP, p.42). Christ manifested the divine spirit in perfect form. Whether the spiritual realizations of Christ, Krishna, or Buddha were different is insignificant in this context. When the Dalai Lama takes refuge in Buddha, when Rudolf Steiner sees the Christ as central to the development of mankind, they merely exemplify different traditions and preferences but there are no fundamental differences. The reincarnated Lama, in his spiritual greatness, does not deny his respect to the Christian and the Anthroposophist is not arrogant enough to want to convert the Tibetan Buddhist. What all of them have in common, however, is that they regard Christ as a divine messenger who, in community with other perfect beings, with masters and initiates, guides spiritual development on earth. As the living, resurrected, cosmic Christ, he can be perceived by the opened eye of the seer and His blessings fill the earthly realm and the inner worlds. Having completed His evolution on earth, the path will continue for us all— even for Him. We shall all rise toward newer, more splendid worlds and tasks. No created being (Esoteric Philosophy does not see Christ as *non-conceived* or *non-created*) will ever achieve the perfection of the absolute God.

Today's Benedictine mythology displays an interpretation of the teachings on the Trinity closely resembling this esoteric point of view. The Trinity is understood as a cosmic mystery, whereby the Father is the source of Being, the Son represents all that has been created, and the Spirit connects the Son again with the Father. For the great Benedictines Henri Le Saux (Swami Abhishiktananda) and Bede Griffiths, the Advaita-Vedanta influenced this particular context considerably. In both men's search and teachings, they combined Indian and Christian mysticism, wherein the 'inner Christ,' the 'soul spark' in the sense of Meister Eckhart, plays a determining role.

At this point, mystical theology and Esoteric Philosophy touch one another. They eventually merge into the great stream of wisdom. Similarly, Rudolf Steiner said that each individual must give birth to the Christ within, to carry the "claim to the Christ" in his heart.

The esoteric traditions consider the teachings of the Church concerning the Trinity tragic in two respects: one, the deification (not the worship!) of Christ, and two, the making absolute of the *one* incarnation. The first breaks Christ from the process of evolution, de-humanizing Him and so rendering the "imitation of Christ" impossible. For every other being, it becomes a hopeless task from the very outset. The second discriminates against all other divine messengers, prior to and following Christ, and destroys any form of religious dialogue. History is filled with painful documentation of this effect. Only in more recent times and based upon a modified image of Christ (due largely to Hans Küng) has the religious dialogue between Islam and Christianity seen any revival, even on the part of 'official' representatives.

Only when the living, cosmic Christ once more becomes the divine brother who, resplendent among his divine siblings, calls on his younger earthly brothers and sisters, can He fulfill His work. Only then can He be reborn in the heart and only then can the way lead through Him to the Father.

CHAPTER 7

The Creation of Mankind

God is love, but love cannot be perfect as long as it is without an object into which it can pour itself and which responds.

CHARLES W. LEADBEATER

"*Man is the summit* of the Creator's work." (§343)

"The Church teaches that every spiritual soul is created immediately by God—it is not 'produced' by the parents—and also that it is immortal: it does not perish when it separates from the body at death, and it will be reunited with the body at the final Resurrection." (§366)

The question of the creation of humankind touches on many aspects, to be addressed in detail later and within other contexts. There are two essential central differences.

In Esoteric Philosophy, humanity definitely is not the "summit of the Creator's work" and the *human* soul is not "created immediately by God." The esoteric understanding of creation functions within entirely different dimensions than the biblical-theological concept. It designs an enormous panorama of universes and worlds, which are coming into or passing out of existence. The first volume of *The Secret Doctrine* by H. P.

Blavatsky, or *An Outline of Occult Science* by Rudolf Steiner are attempts to put into words that which surpasses human comprehension. The human observer falls silent in awe before the majesty of the visible universe—the seer is even more awestruck before the divine realms his seeing eye beholds.

Life is born from the divine Being, like a divine spark, an angelic seed. This divine spark, not yet conscious, descends through infinite passages, growing and ripening, fulfilling the divine idea slumbering within, to meet its eternal destiny. What once was born unconsciously from the Divinity shall one day return as a conscious child of God, to work in unity with the Oneness, in freedom and complete harmony.

A human being represents merely an interim existence and, looking back, each individual recognizes part of the path he or she has traveled, with a heart filled by an intuition of the glorious future that awaits.

The spiritual soul is indeed immortal—an understanding where esoteric teachings agree with those of the Catholic Catechism. However, when the soul takes a human form it has already traveled far and will frequently return to the earthly realm. 'Resurrection' occurs with every death, when freed again from the earthly form taken to live out its experiences on this earthly realm. It will not wait for 'Judgment Day' to be re-united with one of its earthly bodies. These would have long turned to dust while the spiritual soul continues along its path. It does not live again and again along the same repetitive ground; *it travels farther,* progressing along the path with each incarnation.

CHAPTER 8

The Fall of the Angels

It appears that the transformation of a divine spark into an individual human form with all the possibilities available on the super-human levels— where absolute freedom is joined in full conscious unity with the divine origin—is attainable only in that the divine nucleus, the budding consciousness, develops from a state of complete ignorance into a state of omniscience. Freedom must apparently be developed with no association to memory, since each memory represents a limitation to freedom.

SRI RAM

"Scripture speaks of a sin of these angels. This 'fall' consists in the free choice of these created spirits, who radically and irrevocably *rejected* God and his reign. We find a reflection of that rebellion in the tempter's words to our first parents: 'You will be like God.' [Gen. 3:5] The devil 'has sinned from the beginning'; [1 John 3:8] 'he is a liar and the father of lies.'" [John 8:44] (§392)

"It is the *irrevocable* character of their choice, and not a defect in the infinite divine mercy, that makes the angels' sin unforgivable." (§393)

The esoteric traditions know two models regarding the teachings on evolution, one of which is closer than the other to the Catholic belief. The primary question is about the process of gaining consciousness. Were the *divine sparks* supposed to go all the way down into matter (the involution model)? This would place humans in the position of arriving at the lowest point of a long cosmic journey. Or was the material plane—in this case our earth—the result of a 'cosmic decline' (the model of the fallen angels)?

The controversial debate of involution versus decline is as old as humanity itself. Records span the Gnostic-hermetic writings, traditional stories of mysteries, and the myths and legends of cultures long past. These records debate whether the body is the price of sin or whether it is the gift of the Gods.

Speaking generally, one cannot reconcile God's mercy and kindness with a depiction in which some beings tumble into the darkness as the 'poor misled.' A 'decline' can only be an event resulting from an incorrect decision made from a position of personal freedom. It is also entirely unacceptable that such an event is of "irrevocable character," and that therefore "the sin of the angels cannot be forgiven." No finite event creates infinite consequences.

All movement, no matter in what spheres or worlds it takes place, occurs in freedom. One must experience this free choice, in a certain respect, without conscious ties to the divine source. The price for this freedom may be an action that *defies* divine wisdom. However, without such freedom all forms of life remain, as it were, divine puppets.

Hence, criticism from the point of view of Esoteric Philosophy, if it favors the 'decline model' of the teachings of the Catholic Catechism, relates to the two determining factors: temptation and punishment. There was no 'chief devil' (chief angel) who tempted unknowing creatures, causing their fall; there is no eternal damnation resulting from a possible offense to the divine plan of evolution. Moreover, all events relate only to a small segment of universal life. The material world may appear enormously vast, yet in the all-encompassing being of God it represents merely a tiny drop in the ocean of life.

Again, the staggeringly unmerciful attitude of a Church pretends to speak in the name of love but allows the concept of eternal damnation readily to pass its lips. All beings were, are, and will safely remain in God's omnipotence and shall someday live again in complete harmony with the "Lord of Being."

CHAPTER 9

Original Sin

I came to live in the shimmer of love and in the light of beauty. Both are reflections of God.

KAHLIL GIBRAN

"All men are implicated in Adam's sin..." (§402)

"Following St. Paul, the Church has always taught that the overwhelming misery which oppresses men and their inclination toward evil and death cannot be understood apart from their connection with Adam's sin and the fact that he has transmitted to us a sin that we are all born afflicted, a sin which is the 'death of the soul.'" (§403)

"By yielding to the tempter, Adam and Eve committed a *personal sin,* but this sin affected *the human nature* that they would then transmit *in a fallen state.* It is a sin which will be transmitted by propagation to all mankind, that is, by transmission of a human nature deprived of original holiness and justice. And that is why original sin is called 'sin' only in an analogical sense: it is a sin 'contracted' and not 'committed'—a state and not an act." (§404)

47

The idea of a "contracted" sin is quite foreign to Esoteric Philosophy, which, as a matter of principle, emphasizes the individual responsibility of each being. (Please note that since the time of Augustinus, there has been a close tie between sin and sexuality in the teachings of the Church!) Each individual is fully responsible for his or her own fate. The idea of trying to explain a newborn's hopeless fate due to "Adam's sin" is completely unacceptable.

What kind of justice is presumed to rule the Catholic God who permits human suffering and misbehavior in the Twentieth Century as a result of Adam's sin? Has the thief or liar (whose soul—according to Catholic belief—God created at the beginning of his incarnation) become what he is merely because of his bad "inheritance?" An individual might die at the age of thirty-five—shot to death while committing a bank robbery. Who shall have the right to condemn him to eternal damnation on Judgment Day? According to the model of original sin, one is liable merely in a very conditional way since the original debt rests with Adam. All this is in spite of the problem that this kind of thwarted divine reproduction of souls must be quite imperfect, looking at the world as it is today.

To what extent Adam deserves damnation in this chain of thought is debatable, for how should he and Eve have been able to resist the spiritually far more advanced "serpent?" They were at a severe disadvantage from the start and the 'catastrophe' was inevitable. According to the Catholic model, one might question whether God had *negligently* risked the entire human evolution. One should ask of the Catholic theology through what biological genetic component does one inherit the original sin. The Church makes excuses for the missing explanation as to how the original sin is genetically inherited, though this concept is of central dogmatic significance. The Pope emphasized it *explicitly* [see JP, p.85], and it has already triggered a profound lack of understanding and doubt. However, that humanity should suffer for a sin it has inherited, rather than committed, brings even greater discomfort.

The esoteric teachings support the idea of karma rather than the teachings of original sin. One's every action entails a corresponding reaction—as the cause, so the effect. Everyone's fate corresponds to those seeds sown in the past. The law of karma works infallibly; not a hair falls from a starling's head absent the Divine will. Talents and frailties in character, illness and health, good luck and suffering, all correlate to the individual's karma. Karmic law watches over world justice and humanity is not punished *for* its sins—by a punishing God— but *by* them. In German, the word "sin" derives from the word meaning *to separate*. The sinner has separated himself from God.

As long as an individual *lives by the law,* he is subject to karmic justice. It is only possible for one to undo karmic debt, and so find the way back to the Light, if an individual lives by love.

At the end of the path stands the redeemed being who shall reap neither good nor bad karma but who shall work in complete freedom, in harmony with divine love.

CHAPTER 10

Christ's Redeeming Work

*The difference between Christ and His less evolved
brothers is a difference in degree, not in essence.
All are essentially "of one essence with the Father,"
yet not all are...as He is, consciously one with the
Father.*

CHARLES W. LEADBEATER

"...and it is Christ alone who teaches—anyone else teaches to
the extent that he is Christ's spokesman, enabling Christ to teach
with his lips..." (§427)

"It is the divine name [Jesus] that alone brings salvation..."
(§432)

"Jesus calls himself the 'only Son of God,' [John 3:16] and by
this title affirms his eternal preexistence." (§444)

"...for the Father handed his Son over to sinners in order to
reconcile us with himself." (§614)

No seeker, no disciple on the path, no student of any esoteric
tradition will ever question the spiritual greatness of Christ—
but none will consider Him to be the "only Son of God" either.
Christ was a wonderful divine messenger, possibly the most

magnificent light ever to shine on this earth, bearing witness to the greatness of the Highest—but He was not the only teacher. Every initiate or enlightened mystic reveals truth, regardless of which religious tradition he or she follows. The true connection to the Inner Light, the Divine Spirit, offers a guarantee for true teachings—and it is not limited to the Christian path, let alone that of the Catholic Church.

Without doubt Jesus gave us a *unique* message of salvation but not the only one. Many paths lead into the light. However, the Pope delivers a very different message: "Nor is there any other name [than Christ] under heaven given to the human race by which we are to be saved." (JP, p.30) In my view, considering all other paths to be false—or at the very least inferior— reflects an attitude of both profound spiritual ignorance as well as arrogance.

The esoteric traditions do not question Christ as a Son of God. However, they do question the uniqueness of this event. Through His work and His spiritual greatness, Christ was re-born into God's Light, to reveal God's Splendor through Himself, but one day all humans shall experience their rebirth as sons and daughters of God. If Christ was the firstborn of human children then He was so in an evolutionary sense, not in any essential way different from all of His other brothers and sisters on earth. The phrase *quasi unigeniti a patre* translates in John's prologue, as "a father's only Son" (John 1:14). The apostles followed Jesus 'reborn of God' with an inner certainty that they were "gods, children of the Most High." (Psalm 82:6, John 10:34)

Esoteric Philosophy questions the idea that God has to be appeased—much less that a bloody sacrifice of His "only Son" is a requirement for this purpose. To wise and knowing men and women this idea represents a perversion of the image of a loving God. What kind of God would it be who rages, who takes offense, and who needs appeasement? How could the image of God, who is omnipotent, all-kindness, and all-love, be so distorted?

God's love embraces all of life from eternity to eternity. Through sin (separation) a being can separate and split itself from the blessings of this love, yet love continues to exist eternally. As soon as the individual opens himself for the love, he or she will live in the realm of grace and love once more. This requires no appeasement and certainly no sacrifice to happen. A god who demands a (human) sacrifice for appeasement is no more than an idol.

CHAPTER 11

Peter

The kings of the Gentiles exercise lordship over them; and they that exercise authority upon them are called benefactors. But ye shall not be so: but he that is greatest among you, let him be as the younger; and he that is chief, as he that doth serve.

JESUS OF NAZARETH (LUKE 22:25-26)

"The power to 'bind and loose' connotes the authority to absolve sins, to pronounce doctrinal judgments, and to make disciplinary decisions in the Church. Jesus entrusted this authority to the Church through the ministry of the apostles and in particular through the ministry of Peter, the only one to whom he specifically entrusted the keys of the kingdom." (§553)

"The Lord made Simon alone, whom he named Peter, the 'rock' of his Church." (§881)

In these quotations the Roman Catholic Church speaks of itself, manifesting its claim to power. Rome, and only Rome, "binds" and "looses." It does all this in the name of one whose kingdom is not of this world.

The debate as to whether Peter was ever in Rome is an old one and still remains inconclusive. What is certain, however, is that the entire New Testament has no knowledge of any Bishop of Rome and the first real Bishops of Rome did not consider themselves to be Popes. Even as late as in the Fifth Century, the Council of Chalcedon decreed the equality of the Bishops of Rome and the Bishops of Constantinople. Nevertheless, from the very beginning the Catholic Church declared its papal legitimacy as ordained by God and so valid from the very outset. As Küng pointed out recently, from a historic perspective this is more than doubtful, taking into account current research. Esoteric teachings have always argued that this claim was never the intention of Jesus of Nazareth. For them, the essence of the religious teachings is mainly service and brotherly love. The wise teaches the disciple to find his or her true divine nature and own divine destiny in full freedom. The master never claims power over his or her students, nor demands the right to judge them. Neither may the master "bind" them to or "loose" them from their own personal responsibilities.

A teacher is the disciple's light in the darkness. He opens the opportunity for the disciple to participate in his wisdom, without turning this wisdom into dogma and without declaring it to be obligatory. This is true for all esoteric traditions, encompassing a world view with many facets, which is neither *obligatory* as a whole nor in its individual aspects. The mystic path knows but freedom of the spirit, there is no room for papal authority but only a place for companions on the journey, friends and fellow-seekers who share their wisdom with one another.

Sri Aurobindo gave possibly the most beautiful description of a spiritual teacher, master, or Guru in the context of his Integral Yoga. These far-reaching words confront the *power of the Church* with the *child among children:* "This, too, shall be a characteristic of the teacher of Integral Yoga—that he will not for his own sake, nor for human vanity, nor to satisfy his ego, make any claims to be a Guru. If he has work to do, he was entrusted with this work from above. He himself is a channel, a carrier, a representative. He is a human being helping his brothers; a child leading children, a light kindling other lights, an awakened soul awakening other souls."

CHAPTER 12

The Resurrection

When a man dies, the etheric part of his physical body withdraws from the body's denser matter. Briefly thereafter, the astral body separates itself from the etheric body and life of a human on the astral plane has begun .

CHARLES W. LEADBEATER

"By means of touch and the sharing of a meal, the risen Jesus establishes direct contact with his disciples…Yet at the same time this authentic, real body possesses the new properties of a glorious body: not limited by space and time but able to be present how and when he wills…" (§645)

"The truth of Jesus' divinity is confirmed by his Resurrection." (§653)

It is difficult to fathom why the resurrection of the God Jesus needs any kind of confirmation. The religious traditions speak of numerous figures who were resurrected and who ascended to heaven. It is also not unique to find that the resurrected are no longer subject to space and time. In the esoteric traditions it is also a well-known phenomenon that resurrected souls might use their old physical bodies later on to envelope the more subtle matter of their beings, to show themselves to the physical world in this familiar form. To conclude from such a resurrection that life-after-death *must* take place in the limited form of the old physical body is to be misled.

In general, the deceased leaves his physical body behind and is clothed in subtler matter as he enters into the spiritual realms. In the case of Christ, a transformation of the physical body might have occurred as well, since His body, already completely spiritualized during His life as Jesus of Nazareth, was no longer subject to the laws of nature. This, however does not legitimize the strange emphasis on the *physical body* as employed by the Catholic Church, which has tremendous difficulties with the concept of the existence of the soul as subtle matter in her teachings on life-after-death.

Esoteric teachings explain that the physical form decomposes after death while the spirit-soul rises into higher spheres, continuing to exist as an individual, without the need for a physical shell that corresponds to its now-discarded material body.

Contrary to this understanding, the Catholic Catechism states: "The 'resurrection of the flesh' (the literal formulation of the Apostles' Creed) means not only that the immortal soul will live on after death but that even our 'mortal body' will come to life again." (§990)

As to when this mysterious resurrection of the flesh will occur, the Catholic Catechism does not provide an answer or defers the answer to an unspecified point in time, such as on the "day of resurrection" (§1005), or on the "Christ's Parousia," i.e., the return of Christ (§1001). Will the resurrected Christ then appear in the body he carried as Jesus of Nazareth?

The *cosmic Christ* in the spiritual world is unlikely to carry a scar-covered crucified body simply to demonstrate the resurrection of the physical body. Life-after-death is more likely to greet a body of subtler matter which then, according to its maturity, is drawn into those spheres to which it corresponds. Christ ascended to the splendor of divine spheres, from where He inspires the evolution of the earth.

Chapter 13

Ecumenism

There is only one God—the Creator of all things.
And man's true religion is to search for Him.

YOGANANDA

"For it is through Christ's Catholic Church alone, which is the universal help toward salvation, that the fullness of the means of salvation can be obtained." (§816)

"But we must realize 'that this holy objective—the reconciliation of all Christians in the unity of the one and only Church of Christ—transcends human powers and gifts.'" (§822)

"But 'there never is an ecumenical council which is not confirmed or at least recognized as such by Peter's successor.'" (§884)

As before, the tragic connection between absolutist claims and power becomes evident once again. While for esoteric traditions truth and salvation may be found on numerous paths, Rome recognizes it only within the Catholic Church. Other Christian Churches may obtain salvation indirectly at best. That is, only through the power that manifests itself within the Catholic Church [see §819]. On the basis of this autocratic perception, the Pope points out in his book that the Christian unity can occur only under the roof of the "one Church—the only one capable of speaking in His name" (JP, pp.144-145), which for John Paul II means the Roman Catholic Church. It seems to be that in his view it is never the Catholic Church preventing a dialogue, for she already carries the truth and salvation. Rather, it becomes the duty of all other denominations to make an effort to return to their origin.

In §884 it is stated clearly how and when ecumenism is possible: "There never is an ecumenical council which is not confirmed or at least recognized as such by Peter's successor." (§884) Therefore, it seems to be obvious that at least under the present Pope's rule there will be none.

It remains unclear what kind of 'ecumenism' is sought for in some Roman offices. It must vacillate somewhere between affiliation, annexation and unconditional surrender.

To reach a true dialogue, as desired among the followers of esoteric traditions, Catholic absolutism has a long way to go. This contrast become even more evident when one considers ecumenism in the world religions.

CHAPTER 14

Rome and the World Religions

All religions are true, they are nothing but different paths to the same God.

RAMAKRISHNA

"The Jewish faith, unlike other non-Christian religions, is already a response to God's revelation in the Old Covenant." (§839)

"The Catholic Church recognizes in other religions that search, among shadows and images, for the God who is unknown yet near since he gives life and breath and all things and wants all men be saved." (§843)

"The social duty of Christians is to respect and awaken in each man the love of the true and the good. It requires them to make known the worship of the one true religion which subsists in the Catholic and apostolic Church. Christians are called to be the light of the world." (§2105)

Paragraphs §839, §843 and §2105, which could be substituted by numerous others, display a disrespect for non-Catholic spirituality and go hand in hand with a fixated idea of being the 'chosen one.' The 'recognition' of Judaism as a "response" to

God's revelation is almost a mockery when we regard the history of the Christian-Jewish relationship and the legend of the "guilt for Christ's death."

Even though esoteric traditions may be critical of the self-chosen circumscription of orthodox Judaism, they bow respectfully to initiated Cabbalists, to the great Rabbis and Zaddiks of the Chassidic Tradition. Jewish mysticism has enriched traditional wisdom to an extraordinary degree and has made a special contribution to the unshakable reverence toward the uniqueness of an absolutely transcendent and omnipotent God.

In the Catholic Catechism, where Judaism is considered a mere spiritual predecessor, the followers of other religious orders are classified as "seekers among shadows and images." Kabir and Rumi, Shankara and Sri Aurobindo, Gandhi and the Dalai Lama, along with numerous other great sages and mystics, are merely seekers among shadows!

Esoteric Philosophy emphatically denies the Catholic Church's claim manifested in quotes such as the ones above. The same applies to the Pope's remarks regarding Buddhism [see JP, pp.21, 43, 84-90], which do not reflect a true understanding on the matter. The works of a Lama A. Govinda, D.T. Suzuki, or the Dalai Lama do not seem to have been studied by the Vatican. To still speak of the "one true religion" after two thousand years of 'Christian' history can only be understood as arrogance.

Of course, Christians are called on to be the light of the world but should the goal not be to realize Christ's light within one's own heart? Rather, the Catholic Catechism encourages its followers to be missionaries for the Roman Catholic Church.

Moreover, the enigmatic statements in the Catechism regarding religious freedom are more than questionable. For example, religious liberty does not give "the moral license to adhere to error, nor a supposed right to error." (§2108) These statements exemplify a form of self-righteousness by an organization that, fortunately, does not wield complete power over institutions in a secular and informed society—although there are certainly more than enough orders and congregations in the world who apply all their strength to overcome this perceived 'deficit.'

The esoteric traditions welcome all seekers from all religious traditions and invites them to introduce their realizations and insights into the great religious discussion. However, they most emphatically reject *any* claims to absolutism by any orthodox-fundamentalist religious group. God's light shines on all men and women and illuminates all hearts which are pure and open, no matter whether in the East or in the West. No matter whether the name that is called upon be Krishna or Christ, Buddha or Jehovah. The name is but sound and smoke; what counts is the love in one's heart.

CHAPTER 15

Infallibility

The moment one follows somebody, one stops following the truth.

KRISHNAMURTI

"The supreme degree of participation in the authority of Christ is ensured by the charism of *infallibility.*" (§2035)

"'The Roman Pontiff, head of the college of bishops, enjoys this infallibility in virtue of his office, when, as supreme pastor and teacher of all the faithful—who confirms his brethren in the faith—he proclaims by a definitive act a doctrine pertaining to faith or morals… The infallibility promised to the Church is also present in the body of bishops when, together with Peter's successor, they exercise the supreme Magisterium,' above all in an Ecumenical Council. When the Church through its supreme Magisterium, proposes a doctrine 'for belief as being divinely revealed,' and as the teachings of Christ, the definitions 'must be adhered to with the obedience of faith.' This infallibility extends as far as the deposit of divine Revelation itself." (§891)

Pious IX is viewed very critically in the liberal historical writings of the Church. On July 18, 1870 his ultra-conservative pontificate produced, in its twenty-fifth year, the now-legendary dogma of infallibility, unaffected by the fact that numerous high-ranking fathers, in protest of the expected event, had already left the Council.

Within the realm of spiritually open-minded Catholics, this dogma triggered considerable protest and, among other things, triggered the Old-Catholic schism. For many educated Catholics, this exceeded the limit of their sufferance. Those who knew even a little of the history of the Church, particularly the history of the Popes and their 'infallibility,' had difficulty feeling at home under the roof of Rome. For a number of conscientious Council Fathers, notwithstanding the many other errors within the history of the Church, two clearly "heretic" popes (Vigilius and Honorius I) represented an unsurpassable spiritual obstacle.

During the following decades, there were many attempts, e.g., by Karl Rahner and others, to modify the dogma or to qualify its claim. In the meantime, as revealed with the Catholic Catechism, the dogma was utilized to its full extent and with all of its consequences. "Infallibility extends as far as the deposit of divine Revelation itself." That is, it encompasses everything. Since the simple religious follower usually does not even know when the Pope is speaking *ex cathedra*,[†] he must accept all the words uttered by his Pontiff to obligate him fully—which seems to be indeed the intent.

Esoteric Philosophy categorically rejects *any* claim of infallibility. No incarnated human being is in full possession of the truth and one must question seriously and openly whether even Jesus of Nazareth himself might not have erred, in his convic-

---

[†]*Ex cathedra* means the Pope enjoys infallibility.

70

tion about the imminent coming of Judgment Day and the end of time, for example. The problem of "imminence" and of the "delay of Christ's return" most probably refers directly to Jesus and is not a product of the ancient Church.

Having entered the flesh, the spirit is subject to enormous limitations and, knowing this, the esoteric teachings emphasize strongly the need for a free and open spiritual examination of all teachings. "Do not believe simply because the Buddha has said so," said Buddha. This central idea cannot be stressed enough.

No master or initiate is free of error or self-delusion. No seer or mystic is free of inner images or projections that deflect the truth. Even they see in a "dark mirror" and not "face to face"—but at least they admit to it! Therefore, the teachings of the spiritual path place emphasis on a follower's own inner experience. The seeker must mature and grow in order to reach his or her own insights. One may approach the teachers in trust, yet one should not develop any form of dependence on them or on their teachings. One should test everything and then keep only the best. One may err on the path and one may even reject something true and right along the way but in return one walks the path in true inner freedom. It is better to err in freedom than to be commanded by somebody else in servitude. When it comes to the question of inner belief, no one has the right to command another by *obligation* or even *force*. As Raimon Panikkar claims, at the turn of the third Millennium, there can no longer be any more religious obedience: "Even those who believe in an absolute revelation should admit that their interpretation of this revelation is limited and therefore incomplete."

CHAPTER 16

Celibacy

*Who can unfurl his hours and say: "This for God,
this for me; this for my soul and this for my body."*

KAHLIL GIBRAN

"The perfection of charity, to which all the faithful are called, entails for those who freely follow the call to consecrated life the obligation of practicing chastity in celibacy for the sake of the Kingdom, poverty and obedience." (§915)

"All the ordained ministers of the Latin Church, with the exception of permanent deacons, are normally chosen from among men of faith who live a celibate life and who intend to remain *celibate* 'for the sake of the kingdom of heaven.'" [Math. 19:12] (§1579)

It is difficult to fathom how a church that is founded on Jesus of Nazareth could, over the course of two thousand years, discriminate against female spirituality. Jesus' circle included numerous women who might have had an even better intuitive understanding of Him than the men did. Jesus never shied away from conversations with women, which in fact was unusual for a Rabbi at that time. There is no evidence to suggest that Jesus considered women less spiritual, let alone inferior. Men and woman were of equal standing to Jesus—even two thousand years ago.

During Paul's time, the unfortunate then took its course. "Women should be silent in the churches. For they are not permitted to speak, but should be subordinate..." (1 Cor. 14:34) They have to recognize that "the husband is the head of his wife." (1 Cor. 11:3) The man "is the image and reflection of God," but the "woman is the reflection of man." (1 Cor. 11:7)

Thus continues the apostle in an unbearable fashion. In his First Letter to the Corinthians Paul writes about the man/woman relationship in a way that eventually makes a central contribution to the concept of celibacy. "It is well for a man not to touch a woman." (1 Cor. 7:1) After a discourse on unmarried life, characterized by a singularly presumptuous attitude, Paul remarks: "The unmarried man is anxious about the affairs of the Lord ... but the married man is anxious about the affairs of the world." (1 Cor. 7:32-33) Paul leaves no doubt which, in his view, is the more spiritual path.

To this day, Catholic Christianity has not veered from this unfortunate course. To anyone interested in this subject, the psychological tragedies that ensued from this path may be found in the shocking reports by the Priest Eugen Drewermann.

Esoteric Philosophy rejects any form of sexist discrimination. All beings, be they male or female, are equal messengers of God and serve the divine plan mutually. The so-called Planetary Hierarchy, the community of the wise and the sages who direct earthly evolution, includes both men and women. Pythagoras was married, his wife Theano was highly regarded and took over management of the Academy on his death.

In modern esoteric traditions, women have found roles of central significance: Helena P. Blavatsky and Annie Besant in the Theosophical Society; Marie von Sivers assisted at the side of Rudolf Steiner; the "Mother" served in association with Sri Aurobindo; Alice A. Bailey, Helena Roerich and Flower A. Newhouse continued in the theosophical tradition—not to mention the great women who served at the side of such figures as Gibran, Gandhi or Lama A. Govinda.

This is the dawn of a new culture of consciousness—a spiritual blossoming. As its first buds are beginning to appear, it will be strongly influenced by feminine elements. The relatively aggressive male-oriented civilization, dominated by its technology, is in dire need of the devotion and humility of the receptive feminine influence. At the conclusion of the Twentieth Century, the 'female soul' seems to be considerably more receptive to the impulses of new times.

From this perspective, it would be a tragic misunderstanding if men continued to dominate priestly service. Not only is it desirable to see male priests find wholeness through their relationships with women; it would also be of great benefit to the Church and its followers if female priests could serve the Church as vessels for *divine grace.*

Celibacy, as a requirement, lacks any basis in our present age. However, as a free choice, this route is available to any seeker, knowing that he or she may later alter the chosen path through free choice. Should such a promise, often made in immaturity, be of higher value in the face of God than the love in one's heart?

CHAPTER 17

Immortality and Reincarnation

Song of the Spirits Over the Waters
Man's soul
Is like water:
From heaven it comes,
To heaven it rises,
And to earth again,
It must descend,
Moving to and fro for ever.

JOHANN WOLFGANG VON GOETHE

"In that 'departure' which is death the soul is separated from the body. It will be reunited with the body on the day of resurrection of the dead." (§1005)

"Because of Christ, Christian death has a positive meaning…" (§1010)

"Death is the end of man's earthly pilgrimage, of the time of grace and mercy that God offers him so as to work out his earthly life in keeping with the divine plan, and to decide his ultimate destiny. When 'the single course of our earthly life' is completed, we shall not return to other earthly lives: 'It is appointed for men to die once.' [Heb. 9:27] There is no 'reincarnation' after death." (§1013)

The teachings on life-after-death that are outlined in the Catholic Catechism are uniquely ambiguous. Only the soul's reunion with its body on Judgment Day is formulated precisely. The "how" of death's occurrence and the soul's journey through post-death worlds seem to be a blank page for the Catholic Church. The "positive meaning" of a "Christian death" is not clear—never mind the highly alienating effect the emphasis on "Christian" must have on people of other religions in the process of death and dying.

The questionable nature of the dependence between soul and physical body has already been presented in more detail in Chapter 12. At this point, I will not discuss further the esoteric understanding of the soul's wanderings after separation from its physical shell. This topic is too broad to be explained in the course of this brief work. However, a synopsis of the esoteric view is that after death the soul enters a sphere that corresponds to its spiritual maturity. Through the so-called film-strip of life, the soul may re-experience its incarnation and become its own judge. According to its consciousness, it will then remain in the inner worlds for a period of time, as it prepares for another incarnation.

The Church began fighting the concept of reincarnation from its earliest days, a fact that supports the observation that such teachings were spreading rapidly. The Alexandrine Origen, one of the greatest among the church fathers, pledged his commitment to the teachings of reincarnation. This was possible only because his teachings on the soul were clearly in favor of the soul's existence prior to its incarnation. Origen had based his theology on the creation of the spirit. Every spiritual being— all created on the same "level"—may choose to be ever more united with its divine creator, or may chose to estrange itself from Him. Complete estrangement ultimately leads to the creation of matter and to physical embodiment, while partial distancing from God results in the existence of angelic beings. Therefore, souls already exist prior to their embodiment.

This clearly represents a contradictory view to today's accepted views of 'creationism.,' a doctrine that states that God creates each soul when it enters the flesh, and the often-debated 'traductionism,' where the soul is brought forth from the parental substance as a type of procreative product.

Both concepts were rejected by Origen: "All bodiless and invisible reasonable beings, when falling into neglect, gradually glide back to lower levels and take on bodies according to the kind of level to which they have descended; for example, first from ether, then from air, and, when approaching the earth's vicinity, they surround themselves with even denser bodies, ultimately to be confined to human flesh." (De Princ. I, 5:3)

The world of bodies, just like the spiritual world (*kosmos noetos*) is subject to God's justice. Origen tried to prove this point with the example of Jacob and Isaiah: "As, therefore, when the scriptures are examined in regard to Esau and Jacob, it is found that there is 'no unrighteousness with God' in its being said of them, before they were born or had done anything, in this life of course, which 'the elder should serve the younger,' and as it is found that there is no unrighteousness in the fact that Jacob supplanted his brother even in the womb, provided we believe that by reason of his merit in some previous life Jacob had deserved to be loved by God to such an extent as to be worthy of being preferred to his brother…" (De Princ. II, 9:7)

Origen tried to exemplify the concept of karma, the balancing justice, by using the same example. "If we search for knowledge about Isaiah's soul we can find that he was condemned to a lesser status in life, due to former sins." (De Princ. II, 8:3)

Origen maintained that the determining factor was the human soul itself, choosing its life freely. If the soul turned to the logos within, its path led back to God. Otherwise it distanced itself from God.

Origen's philosophy and the philosophy of the Origenistic school (based on his teachings but not always identical to them) would have their consequences. At the Fifth Council in Constantinople, numerous teachings, largely traceable to Origen, were categorized as 'anathema' (banished by the Church). Of particular significance was the rejection of the soul's pre-existence. Hence the first two phrases from the fifteen anathemas of the Second Council of Constantinople in 553 are:

"If anyone supports the invented pre-existence of the souls and the resulting fantastic re-instatement, let him be anathema."

"If anyone shall say that the creation of all rational creatures consisted of minds bodiless and immaterial without any number of name, so that they all formed a unity by reason of the identity of their essence and power and energy and by their union with and knowledge of God the Word; but, that they were seized with weariness of the divine love and contemplation, and changed for the worse, each in proportion to his inclination in this direction; and that they took bodies, either fine in substance or grosser, and became possessed of a name, which accounts for the differences of names as well as of bodies among the higher powers; and that thus the cherubim, with the rulers and authorities, the lordships, thrones and angels and all the other heavenly orders came into being and received their names, let him be anathema."

With this decision by the Council, no further specific condemnation of the teachings of reincarnation or karma was required. If the soul's pre-existence is denied, naturally there could be no re-embodiment, since the embodiment was simply the first beginning of the soul's existence after the soul had been created from nothingness.

In this text, I do not intend to comment on the history of the teachings on reincarnation throughout twenty Christian centuries.[†] However, it is appropriate to point out several basic objections, as raised by the words of the Catholic camp:

Objection No. 1: Body and soul are a unity.

Reply: The body will cease to exist after the physical death, while the pre-existing soul (the spirit-soul) returns to the spiritual world, from where it may incarnate anew.

Objection No. 2: Is it fair that a person be punished without having any memory of the debt from a prior existence?

Reply: Can one speak of justice if one rejects the karmic solution? In that case one is forced to rely on the "unfathomable divine decision." Memory has been erased in wise anticipation, so that the reincarnated spirit-soul can walk its new path unencumbered by the burden of its many historical memories.

Objection No. 3: The concept of karma opposes God's mercy and grace.

Reply: The karmic law is merely a form of God's grace that leads the fallen to new paths, paths leading back to the origin in full freedom.

Objection No. 4: The belief that Jesus, Mary and the Saints

[†] See P. Michel, *Karma und Gnade*, Aquamarin Verlag, Grafing (1992)

have caused their own suffering through former incarnations must be rejected.

Reply: All great messengers of the light can take on the karmic burdens of other beings and so help bring about their salvation (*the burning of karma*).

Objection No. 5: The sin against the infinite God cannot be repented, according to the measure of strict justice, through even innumerable reincarnations.

Reply: This is a completely erroneous idea of God. God does not require our repentance. The fallen creatures require repentance in order to be able to return to God. God offers His hand to everybody and at all times; while some beings reach for it immediately, some may take a longer time (meaning many incarnations).

Objection No. 6: By virtue of mercy, God's omnipotence can enable a human being to mature in a short period of time.

Reply: What is the purpose of an incarnation? Where is the being's freedom when he is a child of God who is 'forced' to mature, so to speak? What would be the criteria for willful granting of grace?

Objection No. 7: Everything that might be explained by reincarnation may equally be explained by the concept of maturing on the journey after death.

Reply: The question of genius and the question of suffering remain unexplained, not to mention the overwhelming mass of material on documented cases of reincarnation.

These objections, raised by Gebhard Frei many years ago, are still often brought forward in this or a similar form but are not very convincing from a philosophical point of view. Hence, the success of the teachings on reincarnation in Christian cultures continues unabated, because these teachings provide sensible answers to the great life-questions of whence and where. It simply is no longer sufficient to stress "the intervention of the evil spirit" (JP, p.61) when it comes to difficult questions.

To close this Chapter, I comment on the central argument against reincarnation in the Catholic Catechism, the quotation from Heb. 9:27, where different scholars interpreted this seemingly clear message in very different ways—a message from Paul, not from Jesus. The priest Günther Schwarz attempted to reconstruct the original Aramaic text. According to his re-translation, it should read: "For as long as man is destined to die, followed by judgment, so long is Christ is to appear to those awaiting him for salvation." In this interpretation, the entire passage might even make a point in favor of belief in reincarnation.

The debate over passages does not enrich the discussion of reincarnation but impoverishes it. The determining factor will be the inner experiences of millions of human beings who feel the certainty they have come from a distant past and are moving toward a bright future—guided by divine love and wisdom.

CHAPTER 18

Judgment Day

To us belongs all of eternity,
to us the children of the universe,
to whom this earth is not mother,
but only wet nurse.

K.O. SCHMIDT

"Each man receives his eternal retribution in his immortal soul at the very moment of his death, in a particular judgment that refers his life to Christ: either entrance into the blessedness of heaven—through a purification or immediately,— or immediate and everlasting damnation." (§1022)

Esoteric Philosophy is also familiar with the concept of *judgment*, although the aspect of punishment that dominates in the World Catechism is replaced by a purely educational one. In its retrospective phase, the soul of the deceased sees its life pass by as if on a film screen but with a change of tone. It experiences itself within those to whom it has brought suffering or joy and thus becomes its own judge. This moving experience leaves a deep impression on the soul, so forming an instructive inspiration. Only after this retrospective process does the soul continue into the realms of the spiritual world, once again according to its level of spiritual maturity. Even though a phase of purification may represent an important experience, the soul does not enter heavenly bliss.

A peculiar aspect of §1022 is that it omits the usual reference to 'Judgment Day,' but a 'normal' judgment is implemented immediately at the end of physical life. While it is not clear in this paragraph who actually performs the judgment, §1038 does clarify that it deals with the Last Judgment. It is stated here that it is Christ who pronounces who is destined for eternal punishment and who will move on into eternal life.

The Pope writes even more clearly: "As a result of this judgment, the just are destined to eternal life. There is a destination to eternal damnation as well, which consists in the ultimate rejection of God…" (JP, pp.72-73) It is almost unbelievable that in 1995 "Christ's Representative on Earth" could proclaim the "destination to eternal damnation." This statement does not require further comment.

As to the conditions after death, the esoteric teachings differ fundamentally from the view outlined in the Catholic Catechism, which the following two chapters will show.

CHAPTER 19

Heaven

Salvation is the fate for all of us, not the monopoly of a select few; no one will be excluded from salvation, since we are all encompassed by the circle of divine love.

PAUL BRUNTON

"This perfect life with the Most Holy Trinity—this communion of life and love with the Trinity, with the Virgin Mary, the angels and all the blessed—is called 'heaven'. Heaven is the ultimate end and fulfillment of the deepest human longings, the state of supreme, definitive happiness." (§1024)

"The visible universe, then, is itself destined to be transformed, 'so that the world itself, restored to its original state, facing no further obstacles, should be at the service of the just,' sharing their glorification in the risen Jesus Christ." (§1047)

Catholic theology recognizes hardly any difference between the spiritual worlds. The sphere referred to as "heaven" lies at a completely diffuse horizon that "is beyond all understanding and description." (§1027) With this in mind, one may find an interface with Esoteric Philosophy—if heaven was an illuminating concept, found at the end of a long cosmic evolutionary cycle. Unfortunately, this is not the case. Heaven and Hell await the lucky or unlucky soul at the end of one single life. Since there is no evolution after death, this concept brings into focus the fearful childish question as to whether heaven is really filled with the song of *eternal hallelujahs.* The image of an infinite richness of spheres and levels, each a home to living creatures of varying maturity and development and all of whom continue in an evolutionary process, is an image that is completely foreign to the teachings of the Catholic Catechism.

One life, one judgment, one heaven! In eternity!

One life, one judgment, one hell! In eternity!

If there is any stark contrast between Catholic theology and Esoteric Philosophy so blatantly evident in a single dogma, this is it!

This contrast becomes even more apparent when this limited vision is applied to cosmic dimensions. The earth and the human race are not the only things caught up in this model of heaven and hell; so is the entire visible universe. Christ is considered the ruler of the entire universe. While the esoteric traditions humbly declare that they cannot envision the monumental size and scope of the solar worlds, not to mention the splendor of the beings in the solar evolution, only seen by divine messengers such as Buddha or Christ, the Catholic Catechism raises Christ beyond all worlds, solar systems and galaxies. The Pope even states: *"Man is the priest of all creation."* (JP, p.16)

Esoteric Philosophy teaches that there are Christ-beings—divine messengers—for innumerable worlds. Jesus of Nazareth is the Christ on earth—*only* on earth. No sage, mystic or enlightened being may more than hint about other worlds or other heavenly spheres. They all feel or see the infinite splendors awaiting the soul wandering on unknown and far-flung paths.

CHAPTER 20

Hell

There is no hell. It is merely a delusion of theological fantasy.

CHARLES W. LEADBEATER

"The teaching of the Church affirms the existence of hell and its eternity. Immediately after death the souls of those who die in a state of mortal sin descend into hell, where they suffer the punishments of hell, 'eternal fire'. The chief punishment of hell is eternal separation from God, in whom alone man can possess the life and happiness for which he was created and for which he longs." (§1035)

In the light of Esoteric Philosophy, §1035 represents the ultimate perversion of the teachings of Christ. In His name, he being the incarnation of love, the Church postulates eternal damnation for *a single* limited, *temporal* earthly life that may have been molded by a harsh fate (karma), for which the only explanation the Church and its dogma offers is unfathomable divine decision. No court on earth would ever issue such a judgment.

If one were confronted in numerous discussions, as I have been, with stories told by representatives of the Church regarding the "infinite divine goodness" in opposition to the "heartless teachings of karma," then §1035 is truly the epitome of hypocrisy. However, at the same time it unmasks an all-powerful Church, which keeps up the scenario of hell to maintain its influence. Why should one seek the forgiveness of sin through the Mother Church if there is no hell?

How many righteous men and women had to die for these irrational, cruel teachings over the course of two thousand years? Origen, the great Third-Century theologian and scholar in Alexandria, was proscribed by a Church ban because of his teachings of Apokatastasis, the belief that every human being, as well as all angels and demons, will ultimately be saved. In *The Book of Heretics,* Walter Nigg has established a moving memorial to all those 'heretics' who, following Origen, stood up for true Christian love and freedom and were subjected to anathema and physical death as a result. Nowadays it requires no great courage to dispute "hell's eternity," yet everyone who casually brushes aside such teachings should, in the depth of his or her own heart, bow to the great martyrs of history who earned us this freedom at the cost of their own lives. Even today, their lives and their sacrifices impute us to continue to oppose those who believe they may stress religion through fear and the threats of hell, as the Pope does in his book: "An even more radical evil is God's rejection of man, which is, *eternal damnation* as the consequence of man's rejection of God." (JP, p.70)

The Christian message must be freed from oppressive clerics who draw dark clouds before the pure divine sun of love. God is eternal, infinite love. In HIM we live. Never can we fall out of HIS love—and how can hell exist within love? No blinded being will ever be 'eternally' separate from its inner divine soul-spark. So all life will again kindle the divine fire hidden within.

Not hell—love alone is eternal!

CHAPTER 21

Baptism

Life is not a problem that needs to be solved, but a reality to be experienced.

BUDDHA

"Every man who is ignorant of the Gospel of Christ and of his Church, but seeks the truth and does the will of God in accordance with his understanding of it, can be saved. It may be supposed that such persons would have *desired Baptism explicitly* if they had known its necessity." (§1260)

"By Baptism *all sins* are forgiven, original sin and all personal sins, as well as all punishment for sin. In those who have been reborn nothing remains that would impede their entry into the Kingdom of God, neither Adam's sin, nor personal sin, nor the consequences of sin, the gravest of that is separation from God." (§1263)

The most successful missionary attitude is to hope that all followers who have not explicitly rejected baptism will eventually wish to be baptized and, therefore, wish to be a follower of the Roman Catholic Church. One may conclude from §1260 that only a person who does not seek the truth has not wished for baptism. A person who, knowing the Catholic Catechism, does not wish for baptism cannot, therefore, be a seeker of the truth.

It should be evident that this elitist concept of baptism is not in agreement with Esoteric Philosophy.

Moreover, the idea that through Catholic baptism all sins are forgiven is in no way supported by social reality. Men and women are still subject to good and bad karma. They do not, by virtue of baptism, add one iota to their gifts or to their good or bad characteristics. In §1264 there is an attempt to account for this; this paragraph allows room for any residual "tinder of sin." How it intended to harmonize these two positions remains unstated; the claim and the reality are blatantly disproportionate.

In contrast, the esoteric traditions of Christian mysticism also know the act of baptism; the spiritual background, however, is entirely different. Baptism is intended to intensify the conscious connection between the physical form and the spiritual individual so that the spirit may express itself physically according to the divine plan. Further, the baptized individual is entrusted into the care of his angel whose spiritual voice is to guide and warn him. The act of baptism should once again promote the spiritual growth of a soul incarnate but does not redeem it from any (original) sin.

CHAPTER 22

The Eucharist

It is Christ who calls every living creature to the
Father. He is the way to the Divine source. Under
His influence we align ourselves with the endless
stream of illuminated energies.

FLOWER A. NEWHOUSE

"In the most blessed sacrament of the Eucharist 'the body and blood, together with the soul and divinity, of our Lord Jesus Christ and, therefore, *the whole Christ is truly, really, and substantially* contained.' 'This presence is called 'real'—by which is not intended to exclude the other types of presence as if they could not be 'real' too, but because it is presence in the fullest sense: that is to say, it is a *substantial* presence by which Christ, God and man, makes himself wholly and entirely present.'" (§1374)

The esoteric traditions respect the sacramental life of all world religions; however, when a ritual is practiced, the spiritual meaning and deeper sense of it is often interpreted differently.

Throughout the centuries, individuals have disputed the Catholic celebration of the Eucharist. The arguments—especially with the various Protestant groups—are well known.

Basically, the esoteric teachings share the Protestants' fundamental criticism; the literal interpretation (eating the body of Christ and drinking His blood) carries strong cannibalistic, or at least ritualistic-magical characteristics. In addition, there is the critical objection that Jesus' words from Mark 14:22-25 could hardly have been intended by Him to be taken literally with respect to His *real* body and His *real* blood, for at the time of the "original" Eucharist He was still alive among his disciples.

Given the background of these justified objections, the esoteric teachings emphasize that all rituals must be viewed from two different aspects. First, the symbolic action expresses the inner connection between two levels. Second, it gives *spiritual* strength to the participants, if they internalize the ritual. When one strips the sacraments of their compulsive-dogmatic flavor, they can present a helpful, meditative means for attuning with a spiritual reality and, at the same time, they offer a portal through that spiritual power may flow to the faithful. In this sense, liturgies and meditations can complement each other quite effectively.

As a rule, it may be stated that most esoteric traditions emphasize the philosophical moment of realization but give less importance to the ritualistic aspect. The reason for this lies in the ritual's expressly figurative character that frequently seems to manifest a fascination with the performance itself, rather than merely serving as a symbol, instrument, or parable. The philosophical individual will realize on his or her evolutionary path that the sacramental aspect becomes increasingly less important.

CHAPTER 23

Penance

Ethics are a kind of teaching which rejects egotism and encourages selflessness.

VIVEKANANDA

"Those who approach the sacrament of Penance obtain pardon from God's mercy for the offense committed against him, and are, at the same time, reconciled with the Church that they have wounded by their sins and which by charity, by example, and by prayer labors for their conversion." (§1422)

How pitiful must a God be who is "offended" by humans—particularly considering the particular "mortal sins" that were a concern in earlier days; some of which remain as such today. A favorite example is adultery. One must ask whether God is more offended by the straying of a Catholic princess, likely to receive a special absolution of her sins, or by a priest's house-keeper, who is more likely to face the harse condemnation of the Church.

In addition, the Christian God was highly angered during the first Christian centuries by any form of "idol worship;" one was guilty of this practice by merely visiting a "pagan" temple or participating in "pagan" rites. This contention is intended to make a humanized caricature image of God, wherever that may lead. True reverence before God's greatness is supplanted by a distorted image of an angry, enraged God, who more resembles an Old Testament monarch than the all-pervasive, all-encompassing SPIRIT.

So in this context, Esoteric Philosophy criticizes the idea of penance per se, as well as the underlying distorted image of God. It certainly makes sense for a disciple on the path to contemplate his frailties in silence and to consciously strive for purification. However, it is of utmost importance that this occurs from an inner realization. A religious priority of compulsive fear under threat of punishment would destroy spiritual growth of any kind. Penance, therefore, should signify *conscious choice of inner transformation,* which then turns to the Divine with a mature, strong soul.

CHAPTER 24

Spiritual Healing

*Successful spiritual healing evokes the downpour
of a powerful divine wave of energy which redirects
him who seeks healing back to the center, and leads
to the cleansing of his aura.*

GEOFFREY HODSON

"The Holy Spirit gives to some a special charism of healing so as to make manifest the power of the grace of the risen Lord. But even the most intense prayers do not always obtain the healing of all illnesses." (§1508)

In theory, the teachings of the Catholic Church and the esoteric traditions are basically in agreement with one another. The reason why the subject of spiritual healing has been taken up lies in the rift between claim and reality.

Aside from the Anglican Church in Great Britain, which practices an exemplary form of collaboration between priests and healers, spiritual healers still encounter numerous obstacles raised by the Church. Over the years, the Church opposed any positive media reports concerning the various methods of spiritual healing. Church institutions deny healers the right to hold seminars in their facilities, even when they are of a clearly non commercial nature.

This type of procedure could be understood if an equally valid offer of healing service was made available by the Church, which, unfortunately, is not the case. On the contrary, priests who feel any kind of calling to the service of healing others often encounter great difficulty from their superiors if they wish to be trained as spiritual healers. Apparently, the Church takes the position that the gift of healing is a gift from birth, a special charisma, which includes any and all knowledge of how this gift is to be used. Unfortunately, this is not a realistic position to take.

Any person who feels the calling to be a healer can learn to use this gift in accordance with the spiritual understanding of human nature. In fact, all humans are imbued with the gift to heal, a gift most of us practice in small ways every day of our lives. In this context, it would be a welcome development if all churches would encourage their members to develop their inherent human gift of healing. Training methods and ethics developed specifically for healers could be created, methods guaranteed to uncover the charlatans who, unfortunately, are present in this field of endeavor as they are in all others.

Collaboration between communities of spiritual healers and the Church could become a real blessing in a society plagued by ever-increasing illness. We can only hope and wish that the Church will remember the gift of the apostles who went out and "anointed and healed the sick."

CHAPTER 25

Priests and Priestesses

The religious mind is something entirely different
from the mind that believes in religion.

KRISHNAMURTI

"'Only a baptized man validly receives sacred ordination.' The Lord
Jesus chose men to form the college of the twelve apostles, and the
apostles did the same when they chose collaborators to succeed them
in their ministry. The college of bishops, with whom the priests are
united in the priesthood, makes the college of the twelve an ever-
present and ever-active reality until Christ's return. The Church
recognizes herself to be bound by this choice made by the Lord
himself. For this reason the ordination of women is not possible."
(§1577)

The radically different position taken by the Esoteric Philosophy
regarding women's spirituality was outlined in Chapter 16. Aside
from the questionable approach of tracing the denial of females in
the priesthood back to Jesus, one must also ask whether all instruction
given two thousand years ago, which was perhaps valid at that time,
can still be considered of consequence today.

During the first three centuries of the ancient Church, women
played an outstanding role in Christianity—in spite of Paul. How-

ever, a degrading and even contemptuous attitude towards women gradually began to dominate Church thinking, an attitude that bordered on the pathological side when, for example, menstruating women were refused participation in the mass.

An open and truly conscious reappraisal of centuries of discrimination against women by the Catholic Church is necessary in order to transform this Church dogma. Women must regain their full honor and recognition as priestesses and divine instruments. Should the Catholic Church continue to try to keep women away from the altar, female spirituality will find other access to priestly work. The strong presence of women among the leaders of the so-called New-Age Movement—from Marilyn Ferguson to Eileen Caddy to Chris Griscom—shows what vitality has been excluded from the Church. With what right was Hildegard von Bingen, one of the greatest personalities of her time, refused access to priesthood and the clergical hierarchy?

The number of publications dealing with critical analysis of a male-dominated Church monopoly is growing continually and the pressure on the Roman Pontiff demanding change will, some day, simply become unbearable.

Esoteric Philosophy recognizes the divinity in all beings, be they male or female, and so recognizes the equal calling to be a servant of the divine, whatever form this may take, healer or mystic, prophet or priestess. A religion that refuses women's work in the priesthood is discriminatory and violates divine love and freedom of spirit.

CHAPTER 26

Marriage

Love one another, but let love not become a bond.

KAHLIL GIBRAN

"Thus *the marriage bond* has been established by God himself in such a way that a marriage concluded and consummated between baptized persons can never be dissolved." (§1640)

"This grace of Christian marriage is a fruit of Christ's cross, the source of all Christian life." (§1615)

"Divorce is immoral also because it introduces disorder into the family and into society." (§2385)

Under the aegis of 'divine' law, the Catholic Church's proscription of divorce reveals another indication of an incomprehensible, dispassionate contempt for humanity. Given the kind of hell prevailing in many marriages, only complete ignorance would demand perpetuation of such a marriage as a sacred law.

Esoteric Philosophy has the opinion that marriage relates to a higher order or that it has a deeper meaning than simple cohabitation. It considers marriage—as well as any unmarried companionship—a karmic encounter of two individuals who have a special relationship with one another. This relationship, not restricted by the organizational structure of marriage under any circumstances, should be lived in mutual love and respect. It is to be a medium for spiritual growth and maturation of the soul. Then and only then is it a sensible form of living. If for any reason individuals in a marriage or in a partnership are unable to resolve their conflicts or tragic past relationships, they should go their separate ways rather than make their lives even more difficult. Disharmony or enmity in marital companionship destroys any basis for the central goal of each incarnation—spiritual growth.

There is no *good reason* to perpetuate a soulless marriage for the sake of social institution, nor does it offer a healthy basis for child-raising, if the children are required to grow up at the periphery of a continuous marital war. In fact, it is much more 'immoral' to continue to subject them to such unbearable disharmony, simply due to fear of the Church.

A goal of Esoteric Philosophy is to help human beings mature morally and to inspire them to be responsible individuals, experiencing freedom on the spiritual path. For this reason and from this base, each individual must be fully responsible for a relationship with the partner of choice. No twenty or twenty-five year old can predict a life-long relationship. People change. Values change. Goals change. Two individuals may go a certain distance together for a certain time, yet their paths may diverge in a respectful way with loving understanding. Although life-long marriage may not always be an attainable ideal, it is certainly not wrong. However, to hold fast to a decaying tradition simply to satisfy the letter of the law or to appease a threatened ego is the least spiritual of all solutions.

The dogmatic command becomes completely unacceptable when it imposes on a couple that is "physically separated" a life of complete abstinence in order to avoid a situation that "objectively contravenes God's law." (§1650) In addition, the Church denies those human beings (insofar as they are Catholics and so already endure a severely tense crisis) access to the Eucharistic communion that might have offered them comfort. They are denied this comfort and—moreover—they are brutally expelled.

This psychological cruelty has weighed so heavily on several German bishops that they requested an audience with the Pope in Rome on behalf of these unhappy people; they might well have anticipated the Pope's devastating refusal.

It requires no special recourse to esoteric teachings to refute this type of psychological cruelty. It merely requires a compassionate heart.

CHAPTER 27

Possession

There is no devil, since there is no hierarchy of evil.
CHARLES W. LEADBEATER

"When the Church asks publicly and authoritatively in the name of Jesus Christ that a person or object be protected against the power of the Evil One and withdrawn from his dominion, it is called exorcism…Exorcism is directed at the expulsion of demons or to the liberation from demonic possession through the spiritual authority which Jesus entrusted to his Church. Illness, especially psychological illness, is a very different matter; treating this is the concern of medical science." (§1673)

More significant than the reference to devils and demons, particularly in historical retrospect, is the recognition of psychological illness. How many "witches" might have been spared horrible tortures and flames if this insight had taken hold earlier? This may not have saved the witches endowed with mediumistic or healing gifts, especially those defamed with ill intent. Nonetheless, it would have represented a step forward if psychic illness had been evaluated differently by the medieval Church.

The field of exorcism, the driving out of devils and demons, is a strange field. In Esoteric Philosophy, we know the real workings of God-defying creatures from the inner worlds. As explained earlier, Esoteric Philosophy clearly rejects any type of devil or satanic image. The esoteric traditions know of a so-called Dark Brotherhood—sometimes referred to as the Brothers of the Left Hand. This is populated by creatures who have chosen the path of Black Magic to actualize some form of titanic pride and egotism. There is no dispute that powerful beings exist in these circles. However, their work certainly does not involve producing a type of psycho-kinetic phenomenon, playing "poltergeist," or uttering profane blasphemies. They work on different levels and it is recommended that this area best be given as little attention as possible.

The beings involved in the Dark Brotherhood would distance themselves from their terrible workings, could they not draw new energies from the evil mental powers of numerous embodied creatures and reflect them on the physical world. Even the horrific idea of a 'devil' that spurs fearful psyches produces a certain type of energy in the inner world. To clairvoyant sight, this may even take on a particular form at times. Perhaps this illustrates what damage can accrue to mankind by its belief in the devil. The consistent and affirmative repetition of such a thought forms a mental energy and it is not surprising that this energy reflects back on the sender. Therefore, a spiritual aspirant will strive to attune himself to the LIGHT, to deprive all shadow beings from their energy source and so leading them to a spiritual rebirth through their own extinction.

More frequent than actual encounters with the Dark Brotherhood are phenomena of possession related to earth-bound beings. Humans who die in a state of mortal hatred or gruesome rage frequently remain in the immediate vicinity of those people who were responsible for their death, attempting to influence them and seeking revenge. This is one of the reasons why Esoteric Philosophy rejects the death penalty [see Chapter 34]. Even drug or alcohol addicted people may become victims of possession-related tragedies when an entity of more subtle matter tries to satisfy its need by taking possession of a physical form.

In any case, this subject should be treated with great respect and left to experts. A primitive belief in the devil, or outdated exorcisms, are quite inappropriate ways of bringing healing to those unfortunate afflicted beings.

CHAPTER 28

The Conscience

The Buddha's teachings say that I am my own master
and that everything depends on me.

HIS HOLINESS, THE XIV DALAI LAMA

"Man has the right to act in conscience and in freedom so as personally to make moral decisions." (§1782)

"Ignorance of Christ and his Gospel, bad example given by others, enslavement to one's passions, assertion of a mistaken notion of autonomy of conscience, rejection of the Church's authority and her teaching, lack of conversion and of charity: these can be at the source of errors of judgment in moral conduct." (§1792)

"Personal conscience and reason should not be set in opposition to the moral law or the Magisterium of the Church." (§2039)

The statements above reveal an unimaginable and deep deceit. Though §1782 grants the individual a clear freedom of conscience, two pages later this freedom is already questioned when one is warned not to engage in a "mistaken notion of autonomy of conscience" or a "rejection of the Church authority." Fifty

---

† Where Giordano Bruno was burned alive.

pages later, the freedom of conscience is non-existent, for the Magisterium of the Church cannot be opposed.

One actually has to analyze the text word by word to recognize that at the beginning of the third millennium a clergical organization is presumptuous enough to subject personal conscience and reason to the Magisterium.

Freedom of conscience, an individual's unencroachable freedom, touches on the nucleus of Esoteric Philosophy. Only a free seeker can truly be searching for the Divine. Only the religion of the heart, unfolding in freedom and love, in true humility and true compassion, can correspond to the esoteric traditions. Therefore, freedom cannot be postponed, cannot be stated as a mere promise to a certain denominational redemption; it must determine the path from the beginning. The Vatican will merely react begrudgingly to this claim to spiritual freedom, for the free individual, guided only by his or her conscience, no longer requires the priestly mediator in order to be "appeased" with the absolute spirit. He who has found inner freedom can free himself effortlessly from external shackles, for "the truth shall set us free."

The esoteric traditions consider that the best insurance against the abuse of freedom is the true realization of love, a realization that should be taken as a guiding line. No one can claim "freedom of conscience" to avoid responsibility if he has stolen from, or even killed, another person out of a motive such as greed. Such an unloving act can never be in harmony with divine wisdom. One who lives within and through love will not abuse such freedom.

Love offers the guarantee for true action. The loving soul will be the invincible warrior on freedom's behalf; he who has inner freedom will be a shining messenger of love. This is how even today the light of Giordano Bruno and his love shines on the infinity of the worlds, far beyond the Campo dei Fiori[†], while the ashes of his pyre still blow across St. Peter's Square.

CHAPTER 29

Grace

Grace is the illumination to realize the good.

WILLIGIS

"The merit of man before God in the Christian life arises from the fact that God *has freely chosen to associate man with the work of his grace.* The fatherly action of God is first on his own initiative, and then follows man's free acting through his collaboration, so that the merit of good works is to be attributed in the first place to the grace of God, then to the faithful. Man's merit, moreover, itself is due to God, for his good actions proceed in Christ, from the predispositions and assistance given by the Holy Spirit." (§2008)

If the incentive for free action, and hence the merit in good works, lies with God, then the question arises as to where the incentive for bad works originates. Either all incentives originate from God, or all originate from human freedom. Or, do we have to rely on "the evil enemy" once again?

The American mystic Flower A. Newhouse once told me that *eighty percent* of all human fate is determined by grace. Were humans to live under the *law* alone, the path back to the light would be infinitely more difficult than it has been since the beginning of humanity. If God's love were not always directed anew toward an erring, seeking humanity, we could hardly find the path to the light. This gift of grace from the omniscient is ever-present.

However—and this is the determining factor—it does not undo the law of evolution through reincarnation, which is development through maturation. If God out of grace or love changes a devout atheist to a deeply religious person—and therefore performs a mandatory conversion—why then should He have sent this individual into this incarnation in the first place? Who would even think to suggest that a schoolteacher—out of grace—sends a third grade student to a class of graduates?

When applying these seemingly well-understood common rules and laws to the great evolutionary process, it becomes incomprehensible that grace should contradict the teachings of reincarnation. Aside from a few extremist, law-oriented advocates of the idea of reincarnation, no one would object to the Church's argument that God's grace is forever offered to mankind anew; even over several lives on earth.

Certainly, the possibility of balancing one's karma over several lives on earth is a far more compassionate perspective than the Church's teaching of eternal damnation. Any objection offered by the Church must be weighed against its statements concerning the "merciless nature" of the karmic teachings.

Grace does not void karma; grace transforms it. This constitutes a critical difference to teachings that state that there is only grace and no karma. For, whoever lives outside of love is completely and exclusively subject to law. This relation between karma and grace should not be overlooked.

Esoteric Philosophy understands grace to be the eternal offer of God's love, a constantly flowing stream of goodness. However, His grace does not compel, it does not interfere by transforming; it awaits an opening in the heart in that to bestow its transforming blessings. This universal offer corresponds to a request uttered freely. That is, grace comes only on request. Then it is granted to every aspiring creature.

CHAPTER 30

God and Israel

The Gods from the Veda represent the universal powers, descended from the consciousness of truth which established the harmony in the world.

SRI AUROBINDO

"The one and true God first reveals his glory to Israel." (§2085)

"God, however, is the 'living God' who gives life and intervenes in history." (§2112)

The gulf between Esoteric Philosophy and Catholic dogma is as wide as religious revelations are manifold. Sri Aurobindo's quotation points out this diversity, yet it could just as well have been a quotation from Buddhist, Taoist or any one of a number of other spiritual traditions.

Humanity has always sought after the depth of the divine mystery, where the term "divine" already implies a delineation of certain traditions. The esoteric traditions integrate reverently into their world view the visions of the Vedic seers and the ordained high priests of Egypt. It respects equally Chinese Taoists, reincarnated Tibetan Lamas, love-drunk Sufis, and the wise Cabbalists of Spain. Everywhere that wisdom and mystical experience appear in pure form, Esoteric Philosophy sees and acknowledges the workings of a higher reality.

The Hebrew tradition is merely *one* among many. It is honorable and it guards the secret of absolute transcendence of the one unchanging, almighty God. That is its contribution in the chain of sacred traditions.

Making a jealous tribal God of the eternal "I am who I am," indicated even then a distortion on the part of some ignorant priests. Unfortunately, the Catholic Catechism has adopted this inauspicious idea of God interfering in history, even today. This idea is no longer supported after Auschwitz—even by orthodox Jews. I was assured of this by the former mayor of Jerusalem, Teddy Kollek.

Where such distortions may lead was shown in a grotesque depiction of the British fleet's incursion against Argentinean Falkland Island occupants. The unfortunate soldiers went into battle with the blessings of their respective supreme shepherds. It is easy to imagine whose victory they were praying for. Did they have any idea of the "dilemma" they created for God?

Esoteric Philosophy considers the mystic traditions of all cultures and all times to be building blocks in the mosaic of the great, forever incomplete image of God. It knows that it does not know; it knows it is on the PATH. The greater the idea of God, the nearer to the Truth; the smaller and more fragmented the distorted image of God, the further from the Truth.

CHAPTER 31

The Catholic Faith

Love redeems—thinking does not.

MANFRED KYBER

"Our duty toward God is to believe in him and to bear witness to him." (§2087)

"*Incredulity* is the neglect of revealed truth or of the willful refusal to assent to it. '*Heresy* is the obstinate post-baptismal denial of some truth that must be believed with divine and Catholic faith, or it is likewise an obstinate doubt concerning the same; *apostasy* is the total repudiation of the Christian faith; *schism* is the refusal of submission to the Roman Pontiff or of communion with the members of the Church subject to him.'" (§2089)

Since faith, in a very direct sense, speaks to the religious nature of the individual, a personal comment might be appropriate at this point. To the religious, with whom I identify myself, the term "duty to believe" has a very unpleasant aftertaste. How can religion be a source of vitality if it does not spring from a heart full of joy and love for the Divine You, if one rather considers it merely an obligation? Might this not be the key to the historical tragedy of Christianity, which has forgotten to speak of a "joyful message" (gospel) and that instead has made the obligatory "you shall" and "you must" the pivot point of its preaching?

According to the Catholic Catechism's clear definition, I see myself today as an "unbelieving heretic" who indeed denies "some truth that must be believed with divine and Catholic faith." However, this gives me firm roots in the foundation of the esoteric traditions that fundamentally reject the notion that *truth* be linked to a specific denomination.

In principal, truth is an absolute value. It must be separate from any obligatory connection to any denomination. This does not mean, of course, that a denomination cannot contain truth; it just should not be assumed that a particular religious view is absolute truth, nor should belief in it be obligatory. Something that is not Catholic is not automatically invalid!

In its essential form, the whole topic of faith is considered with strong reservation in Esoteric Philosophy. Anyone—even a person with a minimum amount of historical knowledge—can see the unending suffering that resulted from 'good' faith. One remembers the carnage and tragedy that takes place in religious wars. Religion needs to spring from a conscious *experience* that has borne reflection—whose criteria are truth and a life of genuine love, goodness, and tolerance. Religion that is not supported by these things has caused more damage than good and continues to do so today.

Through the ages, the wise have repeatedly emphasized that we should not accept teachings simply because they have been proclaimed by certain priestly authorities (whatever traditions they may represent). Only after examining his own life path and verifying an idea's purity, a disciple should accept it as a maxim *for himself*. However, one does not need to apply this universally, as the example of meditation exemplifies. During a certain phase of life, it may be appropriate for somebody to choose the path of Christian meditation, while somebody else may dedicate himself to Zen or Yoga during a comparable phase in life—each following an inner truth.

Religion must not be regulated. It must not become an obligation or mandatory commitment. Religion can be alive only when it can develop freely, like a rose in the sun. Faith can release the strength to go on to inner experiences, experiences then being the basis for religious dialogue. When religion, or even worse biblical fundamentalism practiced in its literal form, is used as a basis for religious dialogue, the outcome can be only dissatisfaction, separation, disharmony and suffering. The appeal to dogmatics everywhere must be: "Grant religious freedom!"

CHAPTER 32

Religious Freedom

In the world's present situation it has become especially important to develop greater unity among the followers of the different religions. Such unity is not an impossible goal.

HIS HOLINESS, THE XIV DALAI LAMA

"The duty of offering God genuine worship concerns man both individually and socially. This is 'the traditional Catholic teaching on the moral duty of individuals and societies toward the true religion and the one Church of Christ.'" (§2105)

"The right to religious liberty is neither a moral license to adhere to error, nor a supposed right to error..." (§2108)

This chapter is related directly to the preceding chapter. In §2104 and §2105 alone, the word "duty" appears six times. Regrettably, this unfortunate "duty" is not limited to the 'internal' Catholic religiousness but calls for missionary work [see Chapter 14] for the "true religion" as well. (§ 2105)

The Catholic Church has never fully recognized the religious truth of other revelations. How could an organization that considers all truth to be singly and uniquely anchored in itself understand the profound wisdom found in the *Bhagavad Gita* or the *Tibetan Book of the Dead?* The Catholic Catechism upholds the terrible tradition of Roman claims to absolutism and, therefore, excludes itself from the dialogue of the world religions. It seems that Rome does not want to discuss; Rome wants to continue its mission. Rome does not want the search for truth through dialogue; Rome is striving for power.

Therefore, the basic difference between Esoteric Philosophy and the Church must be addressed once more and in greater detail. No religion can claim the right to absolute and complete revelation. All religions are different rays of the divine light. Together they illuminate the path of the seeker on earth who may then unfold his own religion in freedom.

CHAPTER 33

Esoterics

False learning is rejected by the wise, and scattered to the winds by the Good Law. Its wheel revolves for all, the humble and the proud. The Doctrine of the Eye is for the crowd, the Doctrine of the Heart for the elect. The first repeat in pride: "Behold, I know;" the last, they who in humbleness have garnered, low confess, "thus have I heard."

H. P. BLAVATSKY, THE VOICE OF THE SILENCE

"All forms of *divination* are to be rejected: recourse to Satan or demons, conjuring up the dead or other practices falsely supposed to 'unveil' the future. Consulting horoscopes, astrology, palm reading, interpretation of omens and lots, the phenomena of clairvoyance, and recourse to mediums all conceal a desire for power over time, history, and, in the last analysis, other human beings, as well as a wish to conciliate hidden powers. They contradict the honor, respect, and loving fear that we owe to God alone." (§2116)

"*Spiritism* often implies divination or magical practices; the Church for her part warns the faithful against it. Recourse to so-called traditional cures does not justify either the invocation of evil powers or the exploitation of another's credulity." (§2117)

In both Paragraphs §2116 and §2117, the Catholic Catechism is attacking all esoteric traditions. In what should now be evident as a characteristic approach to dogma, fear is employed as a tool in this context. It connects astrology and clairvoyance with "Satan or demons" and, of course, considers the "hidden powers" to be anything but positive.

There is not a word in the Catholic Catechism about the many scholars—faithful sons and daughters of the Church—who were, and still are, involved in astrology. Over the centuries, astrology was considered to be a recognized course of study at most famous universities. Even the Wise Men from the East were recognized as astrologers. However, Rome's memory seems to be lacking here and there.

There is a hidden agenda, different from what the Catechism pretends it to be. The authors of the Catholic Catechism, of course, are not at all interested in the problem of "unveiling the future." All of the prophesies of both the Old and the New Testaments are no more than prophesies and predictions of the future, prophesies the Church has greedily taken up in order to legitimize its position on this topic. The esoteric traditions have shaken Rome's monopoly of power at all its levels and at all times. Naturally, the freedom of a responsible spiritual seeker clashes vehemently with the way of life of a Catholic Christian who follows the Roman dogma with religious obedience.

The entire spiritualistic movement of the last one-hundred and fifty years has hardly strived for cheap divination; its central concern was the problem of a possible continuation of life after death. This is where the spiritualistic movement has been helpful and, in many cases, extraordinarily comforting. How many people—particularly during the two World Wars—would have despaired of the Church's barren dryness on after-death phenomena, if the spiritualistic movement and, during the second half of the Twentieth Century, thanatology had not given them hope for a continuation of life after death [see Kübler-Ross, Moody, Ring and others]. Rome appears to be completely unfamiliar with the many people, especially with the priests, who have sought these sources of inspiration from their own true religion. It is the deeply religious person, in particular, who is interested in Esoteric Philosophy.

Of course, Esoteric Philosophy is not blind to charlatans who are trying to hide under its mantle with the intention of making a profit from suffering and misery. Some such individuals accumulate great karmic debt this way and the law of karma will undoubtedly hold them accountable for their actions. Of course, the credibility of true astrology is not attenuated by three-line horoscopes in newspapers; those who read cards, tea leaves or coffee grounds cannot detract from the gift of an illumined mystic. Even in the esoteric field, prudent judgment is required, especially as this century come to a close.

To instill fear and to demonize are not means with which to deal with the esoteric traditions; this only reveals the projected fears of those who make such proclamations.

CHAPTER 34

The Death Penalty

For life and death are one,
even as the river and the sea are one.

KAHLIL GIBRAN

"Preserving the common good of society requires rendering the aggressor unable to inflict harm. For this reason the traditional teaching of the Church has acknowledged as well-founded the right and duty of legitimate public authority to punish malefactors by means of penalties commensurate with the gravity of the crime, not excluding, in cases of extreme gravity, the death penalty. For analogous reasons those holding authority have the right to repel by armed force aggressors against the community in their charge." (§2266)

It is strange that an organization that speaks so vehemently against abortion [see Chapter 35] apparently has no problem with the death penalty. Abortion is referred to as murder, although an incarnation has not yet occurred in this case. However, without even taking into account the possibility of error in justice, the Church justifies putting a human being to death.

Esoteric Philosophy rejects the death penalty for two reasons. First, one does not have the right to determine the end of an incarnation of another being; second, it is aware of the danger of negative influence from another dimension by the human being put to death. It is not uncommon that a soul living in a sphere of more subtle matter, often in a state of abysmal hatred and boundless rage, tries to seek revenge on others still incarnate. Such a soul may exert influence over the physical realm through the power of thought or, in extreme cases, through partial or full possession. Therefore, it is naive of those who favor the death penalty to think "dead is dead" and the problem is taken care of.

"Life and death are one," as the wise poet Kahlil Gibran has his *Prophet* announce, and the forces of hatred and rage and passion and greed do not come to an end with the dying of the physical form. These forces remain unbridled and can exert their unfortunate influence from the netherworlds.

To prevent such a situation, Esoteric Philosophy recommends completely different measures of penalty. It would be desirable to introduce prisoners to the practice of meditation. This would give them the opportunity to transform and renew themselves from within. When this process has been initiated, socially therapeutic measures or pastoral counseling could be applied effectively and expected to succeed.

Killing a human being represents unwarranted intervention in the divine plan; it also indicates spiritual helplessness and absolute failure.

CHAPTER 35

Abortion

*That which descends from the spiritual world begins
to take effect prior to physical conception.*
RUDOLF STEINER

"Human life must be respected and protected absolutely from the moment of conception. From the first moment of his existence, a human being must be recognized as having the rights of a person—among which is the inviolable right of every innocent being to life." (§2270)

"Formal cooperation in an abortion constitutes a grave offense. The Church attaches the canonical penalty of excommunication to this crime against human life." (§2272)

The esoteric traditions basically agree with the Catholic Catechism on the subject of abortion. Nevertheless, this subject has been selected for critical comparison for two quite important reasons. Although the esoteric teachings reject abortion, they wish to leave the responsibility for such a decision to the parents themselves. Offices of the state or Church should perform an advisory role but should never make such a decision themselves. This is a dilemma that can never be resolved using criminal law.

This brings us to the second aspect. Since the soul preparing for incarnation has not even entered the developing embryonic form, one cannot speak of *murder* in the *legal* sense. From the spiritual point of view, however, the karmic debt to a soul-entity is considered differently. In general, abortion is not acceptable; it represents unwarranted intervention into another being's intended physical life. The karmic responsibility must be faced by the person involved in the abortion, be it voluntary or not.

The esoteric traditions are always concerned with the protection of life and its perpetuation. Inasmuch as they speak out against the death penalty they also reject abortion. However, especially in a field so full of suffering and fear, the esoteric traditions advocate a significantly more kind and loving approach toward those concerned with such a choice, who are quite often caught in a tragic conflict with their own conscience.

CHAPTER 36

Sexuality

*To love is the greatest thing of all, for in it there has
to be the complete abandonment of oneself.*

KRISHNAMURTI

"Married people are called to live conjugal chastity; others
practice chastity in continence…" (§2349)

"*Lust* is disordered desire for or inordinate enjoyment of
sexual pleasure. Sexual pleasure is morally disordered when
sought for itself, isolated from its procreative and unitive
purposes." (§2351)

"*Fornication* is carnal union between an unmarried man and
an unmarried woman. It is gravely contrary to the dignity
of persons and of human sexuality…" (§2353)

Throughout the entire Catholic Catechism, the field of sexuality stands out as one where the leaders of the clergy have
truly distanced themselves from their own basic nature. This
becomes evident when reading the Pope's statements regarding his encounters with love and sexuality during his own
youth, where a young man who "aspired with determination
to holiness," (JP, p.122) is praised as a moral role model. The

Pope's memories of the "young priest Karol Wojtyla" show something rather touching yet, at the same time, incredibly naive. This Pope lives theologically in the Fourth Century and morally in the Krakow of the late Thirties. If not for the *obligating moral teachings established for eternity,* all of this would be humanly comprehensible and quite unproblematic. But today, these moral teachings are rejected as unrealistic, even by the most faithful of Catholics. When reading the paragraphs following §2349, one might think we still live during the Dark Ages instead of in an age of enlightenment. In terms of common sense, it is incomprehensible how, in the year 1994, masturbation is labeled an "intrinsically and gravely disordered action." (§2352)

Rome's comments and renunciations are well known regarding extramarital sexuality, birth control, or homosexuality. All that can be said on this subject has been said before by Karlheinz Deschner in his history of sex in Christianity. Nothing more need be added to his documentation. Hardly any other great world religion has imposed more suffering on more people in its enmity toward the physical body and physical love than the Christian religion. Reading about recent cases, provided by Eugen Drewermann, one knows just how current this problem is even today.

The esoteric traditions have never judged sexuality or ranked the ordinary person lower than the ascetic. Although familiar throughout history with numerous hermits, eremites, or monks retired from the world, they have never considered this the only possible way to enlightenment. However, Esoteric Philosophy does reject sexual hedonism, which robs humans of their dignity by the mere satisfaction of sexual instincts, though this has nothing in common with the "fornication" theory of §2353. Sexual relations between loving, unmarried couples have the same dignity as those of married couples.

Intimate relations between two human beings form a spiritual bond that should not be taken lightly. On a microcosmic level, a union takes place between the male and female aspects of man and woman. This is expressed in the macrocosmic picture of Shiva and Shakti which, in the Indian tradition, symbolizes the completed *unio mystica* (union) of the two polarities of life. This is a spiritual act of immense depth and intensity. Unfortunately, nothing of this is mentioned in the Catholic Catechism.

In contrast and as an example, the *tantric way* considers sexuality as a perfect path to spiritual realization, which may occur when both partners are able to devote themselves to each other's divine self. Unfortunately, Catholic dogma, with its narrow perspective of equating sexuality with a procreative act, denies any spiritual dimension to physical love— never mind the qualities of joy, satisfaction and beauty.

On this topic, Esoteric Philosophy basically favors a *middle* way. An unhealthy form of asceticism no less represents an aberration than unloving debauchery; finger-pointing morality being inappropriate in either case. More significant is the realization that the choice must be realized in full freedom. If someone decides to live in celibacy during a certain phase of life, this person must have the right to leave this path twenty years later, to live in a sexual relationship if he or she chooses to do so. Society can heal inwardly only when sexuality can be lived once again in freedom, beauty and dignity.

CHAPTER 37

Animal Testing

In the temple he found people selling cattle, sheep, and doves, and the money changers seated at the tables. Making a whip of cords, he drove all of them out of the temple, both the sheep and the cattle.

JESUS OF NAZARETH, JOHN 2:14,15

"Medical and scientific experimentation on animals, if it remains within reasonable limits, is a morally acceptable practice since it contributes to caring for or saving human lives." (§2417)

The Esoteric Philosophy's attitude toward animal testing can be described clearly and in very few words. It totally rejects any such heartless procedures performed on creatures under man's care. Animal testing is never acceptable—not under any circumstances.

The tragedy of human behavior toward nature and the animal kingdom is described by the sage Krishnamurti in his journal and so I leave this subject to his care. His touching words, written in a meditative state of mind, do not reprimand or attack; rather they touch the innermost core of human nature. Reminiscent of the Sermon on the Mount, these few phrases represent a call to each of us as individuals. In fact, they also contain a complete manifesto for society. They are words to be received and understood in stillness.

"It is odd that we have so little relationship with nature, with the insects and the leaping frog and the owl that hoots among the hills calling for his mate. We never seem to have a feeling for all living things on earth. If we could establish a deep abiding relationship with nature we would never kill an animal for our appetite, we would never harm, vivisect, a monkey, a dog, a guinea pig for our benefit. We would find other ways to heal our wounds, heal our bodies. But the healing of the mind is something totally different. That healing gradually takes place if you are with nature, with that orange on the tree, and the blade of grass that pushes through cement, and the hills covered, hidden, by the clouds."

CHAPTER 38

Vegetarianism

As long as there are slaughterhouses there will be battlefields.

LEO TOLSTOI

"God entrusted animals to the stewardship of those whom he created in his own image. Hence it is legitimate to use animals for food and clothing." (§2417)

"It is contrary to human dignity to cause animals to suffer or die needlessly. It is likewise unworthy to spend money on them that should as a priority go to the relief of human misery. One can love animals; one should not direct to them the affection due only to persons." (§2418)

Animals have not been placed in servitude under man, but *in his care*. Even in this choice of terminology, Esoteric Philosophy differs from the Catholic Catechism. Most certainly, one would not kill a creature in one's care in order to satisfy one's appetite if it could be satisfied in any other way. This is the basic premise for a vegetarian approach to living. Since it is unquestionably true that a vegetarian may live in a state of health and well-being to a very old age, there is no need to kill our fellow creatures on this planet in order to survive. In addition, it is necessary to consider the aspect of suffering. As distinct from the animals of our world, a plant does not have an 'astral body' that is capable of suffering. This statement should be considered as a suggestion by the esoteric teachings, since it cannot be readily verified. However, it is obvious and recognizable to everyone that an animal senses his imminent slaughter fearfully and suffers greatly in the killing it must undergo, sometimes under great torture. For a freshly picked apple or lettuce, on the other hand, we cannot sense such feelings. Why then should unnecessary suffering be introduced into God's creation by killing animals?

The subject of animal testing and vegetarianism is practically the only subject on that Esoteric Philosophy clearly recommends a specific conduct, albeit agreeing with a Catholic theologist such as Eugen Drewermann. The reason for this explicit direction is that animals do not have a lobby that can intervene on their behalf with the pharmaceutical industry or the butchers union. It is in this spirit that the esoteric teachings must raise a voice on their behalf, asking that each one of us examine his or her conscience to find out if we would be able to personally dissect or torture cats, dogs or rabbits in a test laboratory, or slaughter cattle and pigs at a slaughterhouse. If the answer is no, we should not expect anybody else to do our killing for us, under a veil of anonymity.

Chapter 39

Prayer

Virtue is an emanation of God, a reflection of God's image, which, through its similarity, contains goodness and beauty alone. The soul, fascinated by this magnificent image of all perfection, is driven to prayer by its innate desire for virtue which grows with the outpour of good bestowed by the prayer, so that it will do what it asks for, and will ask for what it will do.

PYTHAGORAS

"Only when we humbly acknowledge that 'we do not know how to pray as we ought,' [Rom. 8:26] are we ready to receive freely the gift of prayer. 'Man is a beggar before God.'" [John 4:10] (§2559)

Tradition says that Pythagoras used two determining factors for the nature of prayer—the soul's voluntary effort and assistance from heaven. Prayer is the mediator, the connecting element between the human soul and the gift of God.

The esoteric traditions generally prefer meditation over prayer [see Chapter 40] without discrediting the value of prayer. A prerequisite for true prayer is selflessness; selfish prayer lacks any spiritual justification. Therefore, Esoteric Philosophy sees prayer as not having any connection with begging. Prayer is related to giving; it is directed toward surrendering oneself to the Divine. True prayer is characterized by selflessness and universality, while false prayer remains caught in the selfish desire to satisfy a personal need.

Prayer also represents a useful aid for the deceased, since the thought-forms created through prayer reach the deceased in form of spiritual energies, to bless and to protect. Thus the here and the beyond are connected spiritually through loving, selfless prayer.

In Section IV, the Catholic Catechism offers much detail concerning "The Lord's Prayer." Two stanzas from the original version are not used in Esoteric Philosophy. The plea "forgive us our trespasses" again indicates an angry God who requires reconciliation. The esoteric traditions principally reject this ancient theology of sin, penance, or sacrifice.

Even less acceptable is the phrase "and lead us not into temptation," although §2846 of the Catholic Catechism attempts to assuage the literal meaning. It is bound to fail when maintaining the original wording. Therefore, the esoteric teachings translate the phrase by saying "and lead us in times of temptation," commanding reverence before God's Holiness, as well as human reason. No one highly evolved would lead a person of his ward into temptation. Such an understanding then should apply much more to the Divine Spirit.

God's love flows in an unending stream on the just and the unjust alike. One who opens himself to devoted, selfless prayer will be filled by this love and will be guided in truth.

CHAPTER 40

Meditation

Therefore the purpose of Buddhist meditation is not to merely sink into a state of noncreation, a state of complete calm and empty mind; it is not a regression to the unconscious or a search of the past but a process of transformation or transcendence during which we become fully aware of the present, along with the unlimited power and opportunities of mind to become master of our own destiny by nurturing those qualities that lead to the actualization of our timeless nature: illumination.

LAMA ANAGARIKA GOVINDA

"Meditation is above all a quest. The mind seeks to understand the why and how of the Christian life, in order to adhere and respond to what the Lord is asking. The required attentiveness is difficult to sustain. We are usually helped by books..." (§2705)

"Contemplation is a *gaze* of faith, fixed on Jesus." (§2715)

The Catholic Catechism teaches that "Christians owe it to themselves to develop the desire to meditate regularly..." (§2707). It must be understood clearly that this particular 'meditation' is nothing more than a form of pious contemplation of Christian content. One of the pivotal points in Esoteric Philosophy is that Catholic spirituality entirely lacks the dimension of meditative depth, which does not mean that it is lacking in individual Catholics. The clarity of this recognition is revealed when an honest seeker such as the Benedictine Bede Griffiths admitted that he had travelled to India to find "the other half of his soul," by which he meant his soul's dimension of meditative depth.

The East has neglected the external world for thousands of years in order to search the inner world and the spiritual treasures. In contrast, the West has concentrated nearly all of its forces toward the external world, thus creating material wealth never before known. It is time for the synthesis!

The West should carry its achievements to benefit the people of the East and then sit at the feet of the sages and invite the spiritual treasures of the East into its heart. The time has come for the spiritually impoverished Christian to drink the water of life again, offered by the great yogis, lamas and Zen masters.

Fortunately, an ever increasing number of people succeed in overcoming fears lodged deep within their unconscious and so open themselves to the meditative paths of the East. The arrogance and ignorance of some Christian dogmatics, including the Pope [see JP, 84-94], becomes apparent when they "caution those Christians who enthusiastically welcome certain ideas originating in the religious traditions of the Far East…" It is as though the God whom a Shankara or Sri Aurobindo beheld were a different God than the One of whom Meister Eckhart or Teilhard de Chardin spoke.

Christian mysticism lacks the door to "cosmic consciousness." In its limiting fixation on the earth and the historical

Jesus, which at most transcends into an uninviting heaven where the saints of all times sing their hallelujahs, Christianity overlooks the inner and outer universe entirely. Where is the occidental seer who, shuddering in reverence, proclaims the infinite nature of the worlds and the eternal ascent to God's unspeakable splendor? This question should be directed to a Christian such as Hans Küng who, although open in general, is strangely intimidated by mysticism and who, invoking "Jesus the non-mystic," continues to emphasize that knowledge must not surpass faith. Küng, in particular, must have realized throughout his many dialogues with representatives of all the world religions that it is the mystic in particular who, due to his or her "insight" or spiritual knowledge, is the true witness of religious dialogue. The synthesis of the religions must first take place on the basis of mystical experience.

Karl Rahner once said in a prophetic vision of the future: "The Christian of the future will be a mystic, or he will no longer be." Rahner will be proven correct!

Bibliography

Benoit, Michel; *Gefangener Gottes* (Bergisch-Gladbach: Bastei-Lübbe, 1993)

Boff, Leonardo; *Church, Charism, and Power* (NewYork: Crossroad, 1985)

Brück, Michael von (ed.); *Dialog der Religionen* (Munich: Goldmann, 1987)

Deschner, Karlheinz; *Abermals krähte der Hahn* (Düsseldorf: Moewig, 1980)

Deschner, Karlheinz; *Ein Jahrhundert Heilsgeschichte*, Vol. 1 &2 (Cologne: Kiepenheuer & Witsch, 1982/83)

Deschner, Karlheinz; *Kriminalgeschichte des Christentums*, Vol. 1-3 (Reinbek: Rowohlt, 1986)

Deschner, Karlheinz; *Opus Diaboli* (Reinbek: Rowohlt, 1987)

Deschner, Karlheinz; *Das Kreuz mit der Kirche* (Munich: Heyne, 1987)

Deschner, Karlheinz; *Der gefälschte Glaube* (Munich: Knesebeck & Schule, 1988)

Drewermann, Eugen; *Kleriker* (Freiburg: Walter, 1989)

Drewermann, Eugen; *Ich steige hinab in die Barke der Sonne* (Freiburg: Walter, 1989)

Drewermann, Eugen; *Über die Unsterblichkeit der Tiere* (Olten: Walter, 1990)

Drewermann, Eugen; *Die Botschaft der Frauen* (Freiburg: Walter, 1992)

Drewermann, Eugen; *Giordano Bruno* (Munich: Kösel, 1992)

Drewermann, Eugen; *Glauben in Freiheit* (Freiburg: Walter, 1993)

Drewermann, Eugen, Dalai Lama; *Der Weg des Herzens* (Freiburg: Walter, 1992)

Feuerstein, Georg; *Gott und die Erotik* (Munich: Knaur TB, 1993)

Fox, Matthew; *The Coming of the Cosmic Christ* (San Francisco: Harper & Row, c1988)

Fox, Matthew; *Sheer Joy* (SanFrancisco: Harper, 1993)

Greinacher, Norbert, Küng, Hans (ed.); *Katholische Kirche - Wohin?* (Munich: Piper, 1986)

Griffiths, Bede; *New Reality* (San Francisco: Harper Collins, 1989)

Griffiths, Bede; *The Problem of Infallibility* (Shantivanam: Ashram Press, 1991)

Griffiths, Bede; *The New Creation in Christ* (London: Darton, Longman & Todd, 1993)

Harnack, Adolf von; *Lehrbuch der Dogmengeschichte* (Darmstadt: Wschftl. Buchg., 1980)

Jonas, Hans; *Gnosis und spätantiker Geist* , Vol. 1& 2 (Göttingen: Vandenhoeck, 1964/93)

Kaufmann, Ludwig; *Ein ungelöster Kirchenkonflikt* (Freiburg, Switzerland: Exodus, 1987)

Kirste, Reinhard, Schwarzenau, Paul, Tworushka, Udo (ed.); *Interreligiöser Dialog zwischen Tradition und Moderne* (Balve: Zimmermann, 1994)

Krämer-Badoni, Rudolf; *Judenmord-Frauenmord-Heilige Kirche* (Munich: Knesebeck & Schuler, 1988)

Krishnamurti, *At the Feet of the Master* (Alcyone), (Wheaton: The Theosophical Publishing House, 1989)

Krishnamurti's Notebook, (San Francisco: Harper San Francisco, 1976)

Küng, Hans; *Eternal Life?*(Garden City, NY: Doubleday, 1984)

Küng, Hans; *Christianity and the World Religions* (Garden City, NY: Doubleday, 1986)

Küng, Hans; *Das Christentum* (Munich: Piper, 1994)

Küng, Hans; *On Being a Christian* (Garden City, N.Y.: Doubleday, c1975)

Lamsa, George M.; *Gospel Light* (Philadelphia: A.J. Hofman comp., c1939)

Lamsa, George M.; *My Neighbor Jesus* (New York: Harper & brothers, 1932)

Lapide, Pinchas, Panikkar, Raimon; *Meinen wir denselben Gott?*(Munich: Kösel, 1994)

Lies, Lothar; *Origenes "Peri Archon"* (Darmstadt: Wissenschaftliche Buchgesellschaft, 1992)

Lorenz, Rudolf; *Arius Judizans?* (Göttingen: Vandenhoeck & Ruprecht, c1980)

Mettner, Matthias; *Die Katholische Mafia* (Hamburg: Hoffmann & Campe, 1993)

155

Meyer, Eduard; *Ursprung und Anfänge des Christentums,* Vol.1&2(Darmstadt:Wissenschaftliche Buchgesellschaft, 1962)

Michel, Peter; *Das Geistchristentum* (Forstinning: Aquamarin Verlag, 1981)

Michel, Peter; *Die Botschafter des Lichtes,* Vol. 1&2 (Forstinning: Aquamarin Verlag, 1983/84)

Michel, Peter; *Leben aus der Stille des Herzens* (Grafing: Aquamarin Verlag, 1986)

Michel, Peter; *Karma und Gnade* (Grafing: Aquamarin Verlag, 1992)

Michel, Peter; *Krishnamurti—Love and Freedom* (Woodside: Bluestar Communications, 1995)

Michel, Peter; *Brücken von Herz zu Herz* (Grafing: Aquamarin Verlag, 1994)

Michel, Petra (ed.); *Wissenschaftler und Weise* (Grafing: Aquamarin Verlag, 1991)

Mühlenberg, Ekkehard; *Die Unendlichkeit Gottes bei Gregor von Nyssa* (Göttingen: Vandenhoek & Ruprecht, 1966)

Origen; *An Exhortation to Martyrdom, Prayer First Principles: Book IV* (New York: Paulist Press, 1979)

Origen; *Vier Bücher von den Prinicpien* (Darmstadt: Wissenschaftliche Buchgesellschaft, 1976)

Panikkar, Raimon; *Blessed Simplicity—The Monk as Universal Archetyp* (New York: Seabury Press, 1982)

Panikkar, Raimon; *Der neue religiöse Weg*(Munich: Kösel, 1990)

Panikkar, Raimon; *Dwelling Place for Wisdom* (Luisville, KY: Westminster/ John Knox Press, 1993)

Panikkar, Raimon; *The Silence of God: the Answer of Buddha* (Maryknoll, N.Y.: Orbis Books, 1989)

Panikkar, Raimon; *The Trinity and the Religious Experience* (New York: Orbis Books, 1973)

Ranke-Heinemann, Uta; *Eunuchs for the Kingdom of Heaven* (New York: Doubleday, 1990)

Rosa, Peter de; *Der Vatikan—von Gott verlassen?* (Munich: Droemer, 1992)

Schiwy, Günther; *Der Kosmische Christus* (Munich: Kösel, 1990)

Schneider, Carl; *Geistesgeschichte der christlichen Antike* (Munich: C.H. Beck, 1970)

Schweitzer, Albert; *The Quest of the Historical Jesus,* Vol. 1&2 (New York: Macmillan Co., 1964)

Seeliger, Hans Reinhard (ed.); *Kriminalisierung des Christentums?* (Freiburg: Herder, 1993)

Thomas, Gordon, Morgan-Witts, Max; *Pontiff* (Garden City, N.Y.: Doubleday, 1983)

Werner, Martin; *The Formation of the Christian Dogma* (London: A&C Black, [1957])

Werner, Martin; *Der protestantische Weg des Glaubens* (Bern: Paul Haupt, 1955)

Wojtyla, Karol (John Paul II); *Crossing the Threshold of Hope* (New York: Alfred A. Knopf, 1994)

Catechism of the Catholic Church (Mahwah, N.J.: Paulist Press, 1994)

By the same Author

Krishnamurti—Love and Freedom

Jiddu Krishnamurti was one of the most fascinating–and mysterious–personalities of our century. Being born a poor, underprivileged boy in Madras, India, he became one of the most influential teachers of our times. Jiddu Krishnamurti's main teaching was to set people free–totally and unconditionally– which is truly a paradigm for the late twentieth century.

In Part 1 of this book, Peter Michel illuminates the most mysterious events of Krishnamurti's life, taking into account recent sources that have not been examined before. In Part 2 he writes about Krishnamurti's teachings, examines discrepancies in a number of records of his life over the years and provides the reader with a complete perspective on the general theme of the thinking of this man.

This book is published in the 100th anniversary year of Jiddu Krishnamurti's birth and we believe that this year will bring even more intense interest in this unusual man. The reader of this book will certainly be left with a rounded and deep understanding of this great teacher of our times.

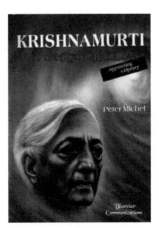

Petrer Michel
Krishnamurti—Love and Freedom
Trade Paper, 208 pages
ISBN: 1-885394-00-4
$10.95